Salvaging America's Black Male Youth

PALMETTO
PUBLISHING
Charleston, SC
www.PalmettoPublishing.com

Copyright © 2024 by Richard J. Fitts

All rights reserved

No portion of this book may be reproduced, stored in a retrieval system, or transmitted in any form by any means–electronic, mechanical, photocopy, recording, or other–except for brief quotations in printed reviews, without prior permission of the author.

Copyright Registration Number/Date Txu000701605/1995-09-05

This book is also available in eBook and audiobook formats

Paperback ISBN: 979-8-8229-5159-4
eBook ISBN: 979-8-8229-5160-0
Audiobook ISBN: 979-8-8229-5690-2

Salvaging America's Black Male Youth

Richard J. Fitts

DEDICATION

In loving memory of my grandmother, Harriet Lafaye Fitts,
my father, Charles Lockridge Jr., my mother, Audrey Fitts Lockridge,
and my aunts Anna Marie Fitts and Marie Lockridge.

I am especially grateful to my wife, Carrie,
and my daughter and sons Marnice, Patrick, and Damon.

Special thanks to Linda Hudson,
'Wale Amusa, and Collette Smith, who edited and typed this project,
and Weston Richards (project manager).

PREFACE

Why write this book? I see no other alternative but to make an attempt at some sort of action plan to alter what seems to be an inevitable revolving door of doom for Black male youth. This revolving door of doom is filled with hopelessness, death, and sometimes self-inflicted pain. On top of all this, Black male youth suffer the slow death of psychological aggression, economic deprivation, and an enormous host of other related negatives real and perceived, informal and legal.

Once I embarked on this project, I realized that Black male youth represent only half of the Black youth population. At this point I was also forced to realize that I was not equipped to address the issues of Black female youth, and I apologize for my shortcomings.

I do, however, send out the challenge of accepting this responsibility to the Black female voice of experience. Just as I am attempting to do from a Black male youth standpoint, the Black female youth issues should also be addressed from a functional standpoint. The Black community has produced a school of psychologists and psychoanalysts whose work borders on pure genius. All that remains to be done is for these works to be organized in a fashion pragmatic enough for its intended audience to use them. This is my intent. To whom is this book addressed? I'd like to answer this question in reverse. Which Black male children, teenagers, and young adults are we talking about? What are their ages? Where do they live?

According to newspapers and daily television newscasts, the crisis-bound Black male youth are first, in an age category from about twelve to twenty-five, and second, they are urbanized. If they are correct in these categories, these youth's parents range in age from about twenty-eight to forty-five. It is this Black parental group that I am addressing. These parents of Black male youth have to decide whether their offspring will be involved in activities that add to the longevity of their lives or cause them to die.

In addressing this Black parental age group, of which I am a member, I want to point out that this book is not an attempted quick fix but merely a start toward addressing a series of very complex problems.

Many are convinced that what we see is an accelerated pace of moral deterioration. I assure you it is not. The severity of the problem has existed for many generations and will continue for many more generations unless we step in and give the Black male youth at least a fighting chance for survival, prosperity, confidence, and greatness.

This book is about the dual cutting edge of commitment. Commitment to our Black male youth, in most cases, already exists. It is its dual nature that we need to understand and act upon.

Commitment, being quite similar to automotive maintenance, gives us two choices. We can either do preventive maintenance and always have transportation readily available, or we can wait until our car refuses to start in sub-zero weather. The next morning we can have it towed, then have it repaired at quite a cost in money and inconvenience. In either case we are destined toward automotive maintenance except that the prior choice is planned, controlled, and prepared for. The latter choice is by default. So goes it with our commitment to our Black male youth. We can either commit to their preparation for a healthy outlook on future prospects and well-being, teaching them all there is to know of relevance, or we can allow them to fall by the wayside, winding up dead, destitute, incarcerated, or in an out-and-out state of hopelessness. If we choose the latter, we will still grieve over our dead youth for eternity. We will still feel sorry for the destitute and help them whenever we can. We will still visit our jailed loved ones, hoping for parole. We will still wallow in confusion about their eternal state of hopelessness. The commitment is both overbearing and present. The only question is whether we will choose a controlled, conscious, preventive, and preparatory commitment or an uncontrolled, unconscious, irreparable commitment by default.

TABLE OF CONTENTS

- PREFACE vii
- INTRODUCTION 1
- WHAT DOES URBAN AMERICAN LIFE HOLD IN STORE FOR THE BLACK MALE YOUTH? 7
- SYMPTOMS OF DETERIORATION (REAL AND PERCEIVED) 13
- FAILING GRADES AND LACK OF CONFIDENCE TO ACTUALIZE THEIR HUMAN POTENTIAL: THE LEARNING EXPERIENCE 15
- DIRECTION FOR THE FUTURE 30
- RESPECTING AUTHORITY 34
- SIGNIFICANT OTHERS AND HANGING OUT WITH THE WRONG CROWD 38
- TIME 42
- GIVING OUR BLACK MALE YOUTH A HISTORICAL OUTLOOK 45
- GIVING THEM THE THINGS WE NEVER HAD 49
- INTEGRITY 53
- RAP MUSIC 59
- PUNISHMENT 68
- YOUTH SAVINGS 72
- DRUGS 75
- INDIVIDUALISM AND HISTORICAL PERSPECTIVE 81
- CONCLUSION 86

INTRODUCTION

How could the Black male youth arrive at such a state of disarray, disorientation, and disrespect as portrayed in daily newspapers all across the country? What exactly is the difference that creates a need for us to make a concerted effort to commit to them? Jews are committed to Jewish youth historically. Germans are committed to German youth historically. Italians are committed to Italian youth historically, and the list goes on. Yet when it comes to the Black male youth, a concerted effort must be made.

Try to imagine us many hundreds of years ago in our own communes, speaking our own languages, and being committed solely to our own culture and ways. Imagine our youth being totally respectful of their parents, neighboring homes, and elders. Envision leadership in the commune being chosen for the commune, by the commune, and by custom. War and violence erupts only when threatened.

Survival and one's lot in life are guided only by those with experience in life and are tempered toward one's well-being and the well-being of the commune as a whole. Imagine the tranquility and peace of mind in just knowing that tomorrow will bring more of the same.

We in our own society were progressing through the historical stages of economic and social development at our own pace. Conceive of knowing who all our ancestors were and of knowing which communes they came from or went to.

We'd wake up each morning knowing that whatever lessons we needed were always available through our parents or other elders whose position in life was to have that knowledge. Specialized knowledge would be drawn from elders and leaders chosen for their wisdom, experience, and the fulfillment of requirements that elevated them to those positions.

There is no questionable dress code, music, or behavior, for it is all by the design of custom and custom's evolution. Sanctions for the violation of these norms are decided upon by the commune, elders, parents, and leaders, all of whom know us and whose only purpose is to give us guidance toward our long-term well-being and the well-being of us all. Rewards for adherence to these same norms are dispensed with much of the same temperament, except that through them we learn joy; joy that is experienced throughout the commune. Religion, education, social life, politics, and economics are all in unison, making our lives well rounded and complete.

Then suddenly one morning, but probably more during the middle of the night, we're all awakened to be captured and herded like cattle toward the shores of Africa. Our captors are perhaps of another continent or of an enemy commune whose objective is to sell or trade us to those of another continent. Some of us get away. Some of us are killed or maimed and then killed, but for the most part many of us are boarded on the slave ships.

Aboard these slave ships we see not only men, women, and children from our own commune but from other communes as well. Captured are prisoners that we know as both friends and enemies, but their friendship or hatred is meaningless, for we are all restrained.

Then begins the long journey; weeks, even months, of lying in our own waste, of lying next to our dead, decomposing friends, wives, husbands, children, and even enemies (who no longer visualize us as the enemy). We are not allowed to speak in our native tongues, which are all that we know, so we are not allowed to speak, not even to our previous enemies. Food and water are just plentiful enough to barely keep us alive. Disease and sickness are all around us and have a guaranteed result: death. Insubordination is sanctioned with murder on the spot or by being thrown overboard to the ocean's predators to set a precedent. We hush our loved ones in fear for their very lives.

After our deadly voyage we land in the colonies that are today known as the United States of America. Those of us that are still alive are weary, weak, and fearful of things to come. In our fear we mumble quietly to our remaining loved ones, and we are immediately separated. Now our young do not even have parents to share in their hopelessness. Anything remotely resembling a family is torn apart.

We are housed in shacks that first night and fed more than we've been fed in weeks, for we are fed the remains of cattle that are deemed unacceptable for human consumption. The next morning, still not allowed to speak in our native tongues, we are again separated into even smaller groups, but this time it appears to be according to our health.

Looking directly through the eyes of our enslaved ancestry, we see many things. Men and women that look healthy, mostly men, are carted away, never to be heard of again, and probably sold. Those left behind are forced, with pain if need be, to work in different fields picking this or that and sometimes plowing if there is no horse or ox. We wished that we could ask the elders or our parents what was going on, but they were either carted away or dead. Sometimes someone in our same position would try to help us do our work or tell us something. If they were caught, they were made to feel great pain in front of us all. Pretty soon no one would talk to us or help us. If we got to like each other, we were separated. If we had babies, "they" would usually take them. If we told on each other, we sometimes got good jobs. Sometimes those good jobs were to make the rest of us behave and do what we were told. Sometimes our women would be missing, taken away for "their" pleasure, probably pregnant now. If our men looked at their women, they were beaten at the least. No one could help us.

They started teaching us to talk like them; it made it easier to understand their orders. If we could talk like them, they let us talk to each other because they knew what we were saying. Still, none of us knew what was going on.

The years began to pass by the hundreds. Now they let us sing. Some of us could read. They even liked some of us, mostly those that smiled a lot or that were lighter than the rest of us. They didn't let us read newspapers, but they let us read their book about their own god and said we could share him. We didn't really want their god, but we forgot all about our own, and there was nobody around to teach us about ours.

Now we all talk like them. Some of us even look like them and will tell on you in a minute. They don't beat us so much no more as long as we work hard. They still take some of our babies and kids, but you might be able to keep them if you behave. We still have to go to them for everything we need and everything we need to know. That's all right though 'cause none of us don't have nothing to give and don't know nothing.

Something is going on. We don't know what, but it's got something to do with us. Maybe it's because some of us broke loose and killed a whole house full of them. It was mostly our young 'uns. They are hard to control and are always ready to kill them and us too if we try to stop them. Sometimes some of us get away and go up North on an underground train.

Anyway, some of them say that this way of life won't work no more. Some of them say that it will and that they will fight change to the end, and they do too. They went to war 'cause they didn't want nobody to take us from them.

Well they must have lost 'cause everybody says we're free. We're free to go. Free to go where? How? Many of us stayed on 'cause now we get paid—not much, but we get paid. We mostly save as much as we can and then go North. We get jobs up North, but we still sometimes have to go in the back door.

Some man was talking about going back to Africa and bought some boats. They stopped that, though, and sent him out of the United States. Another man said we should learn trades, and another man said we should all get us an education. One of us, a lady, wouldn't give up her seat on the bus to one of them, and it really got crazy. Now everybody was marching and protesting, and they were attacking us with dogs and sticks and water. Another man said that their god wasn't our god, and he said he would teach us who our god was and where we came from and who they were. Some of us believed him and some of us didn't. So now there are two gods. Which one is the real God? I don't know. I just know everybody needs God.

They passed some laws that said that we were people too and that we could get some real jobs that paid good money—not all of us, but just so many. Then it got crazy again. They started burning up whole cities all over the place. It was our young ones again. I don't think you can control them. Anyway, after the fires and looting, we really started getting good jobs, houses, and all kinds of good stuff from the government.

Then there was a group that was all over the country that said we should protect ourselves, educate ourselves, and look after ourselves and each other. They had on black uniforms and looked really good. Most of them got locked up or killed by "them." They were the young ones again, the ones they couldn't control.

Things had gotten quiet, and we mostly voted, got educated, and finally prayed. We have come a long way, but we can't seem to catch up with them. Maybe one or two of us can, but they really have to like you a lot. They seem to always be after our males, and one day they beat up on one and somebody caught it on camera. It was on television every day, but the courts said it was OK. Those young ones would not have it. They burned up the city and stole everything they could carry. Then the courts said it wasn't OK to beat us. Imagine that. Imagine all that, from the beginning to the end. Now in the mid-nineties imagine the ones they can't control being singled out for extinction. Imagine that the Black male youth, in his ignorance and naiveté, has made himself quite visible and just as in the past, has nowhere to turn for guidance, support, wisdom, or protection. The Black male youth in urban America will become extinct unless we parents redevelop the necessary traits for their guidance, support, wisdom, and protection. This is their plea, and it must become ours.

WHAT DOES URBAN AMERICAN LIFE HOLD IN STORE FOR THE BLACK MALE YOUTH?

Picture urban American life offering Black male youth fewer and fewer good paying jobs, prohibitive educational costs, and a universal attitude that those blacks should work harder. See job applications requiring experience, shadowed by a heavy overcast shouting, "And you won't get any here." Further down the job application are educational requirements that almost never get met. When both educational and experience requirements are on occasion met, of course they are overqualified. It boils down to the same thing: unemployment. Heaven forbid someone has a criminal conviction, for that would most certainly be against company policy. Feel an urban American lifestyle in which real jobs go to applicants that fall under constitutional documents covering "life, liberty, and the pursuit of happiness." Black male youth job applications fall under documents covering something about "race, creed, or color" (as a percentage of total employment). Now conceive of a historical cycle in which that percentage is periodically debated for removal. All that would be left now are the lower paying jobs. Continue and imagine a minimum wage rising so fast that it cannot outpace the wages of a fast-food chain. In this chain, employment that was previously earmarked as jobs for youth is being usurped by the over-forty crowd. Its management is being conducted by truly trained professionals and college graduates.

This image seems to be one shattering all hopes of starting at fries and working one's way up to assistant manager and then manager. Why should a fast-food chain settle for an inexperienced, semi-reliable, and possibly immature kid when it can have America's best for about the same cost and with a lot less headaches? Never mind that an assistant manager's job may be a real opportunity for an otherwise hopeless youth, especially when it seems all other legitimate avenues are closed. Never mind that offering opportunity in the face of hopelessness builds loyalty. Never mind that the professional and college graduate will jump ship as soon as the next lucrative opportunity presents itself. Never mind that most crimes committed in this country are economic in nature and that otherwise would-be productive employees have had the doors slammed in their faces. Never mind that small-scale entrepreneurs are removed daily from street corners for peddling T-shirts and other nonmajor items in an attempt to secure an honest living.

Urban life holds jails and criminal convictions for Black male youth, jails that are being built with budgets far in excess of the costs required to bring their patrons above the poverty level. Envision jail costs and court costs, which include public defender costs and prosecuting attorney fees. Total up legislative costs that give legality to the other incarceration costs at the local, state, and federal levels. See jails that house a disproportionate number of Black male youth in relation to their numbers in the general population.

Hear social scientists, journalists, and newscasters say out of one side of their mouths that our youth have criminal behavior due to environmental influences. Out of the other side of their mouths they say that our youth are hardened criminals, armed and dangerous repeat offenders.

Never mind that corporate America outsourced the jobs that previously filled its smokestack industries. Never mind the continuous downsizing and restructuring to show quarterly profits. Never mind the union concessions of the eighties. Never mind the massive advertising campaigns that suggest we should all own Buick and Cadillac cars without sufficient legal means to purchase them.

And yet if our youth's integrity slips one notch below sea level, to the jail house goes your son, my son, your brother, my brother, your nephew and mine. To the jail house goes the father of someone's children, completing what seems to be a self-fulfilling prophecy.

Witness, in your mind, the climate to continue such a trend as ever-growing and being fostered even more so by very visual political, legislative, and media personalities. Experience, within yourself, talk with matching laws for provisions for thousands of jail cells and tens of thousands more policemen on the streets.

Upon casual observation it would appear that with all the crime taking place, most certainly there is a need for more police officers for crime prevention, and crime prevention implies preventing crimes before they happen. It follows then that if one is to prevent a crime before it happens, he must always be on the lookout for someone that might engage in criminal activities.

If one has "statistics and facts" that point out who that person might be, then he has a suspect. If he can narrow down the possible suspects even further by using psychological character traits as well as outward physical appearance, suspect identification gets even easier.

Imagine using character traits such as skin color, dress, walk, talk, driving posture, vehicles driven, dress of the vehicle, and anything else typical of criminal peer groups to identify suspects. Now he could support this mindset further by adding all types of hysteria, fear, and preconceived prejudices to the training of police officers. It could be implemented in such a manner that anyone answering these stereotypes becomes a suspect. Couple all this with a centuries-old history of being uncontrollable and you have the ideal suspect. Not only could he make the ideal suspect synonymous with the word criminal, he could also use this perception to push for legislation authorizing all righteous citizens to carry concealed weapons. He could mobilize against the ideal suspect further with a host of police hotlines and neighborhood watch groups (staring through half-cracked blinds with shifty eyes all adding to the paranoia that "they must have done something. They were there."). Understand that due to statistical validation of crimes committed and by whom, the general population could easily endorse this trend. This is the sort of trend that ensures the Black male youth who do wind up in prison will not be locked up with merely other Black male youth. Prisons with murderers, rapists, the criminally insane, and an even wider assortment of cast-asides will accompany our youth.

Contemplate a modern urban lifestyle offering the Black male youth the possibility of self-identity in gangs. These gangs are filled with peers that understand them, peers with the same problems they have, peers that help them achieve the "respect" that society has denied them. Gangs that say to its members, "We are one," that "you belong" and "I belong." Gangs that will allow them to vent their frustrations and maybe get paid at the same time. Gangs that offer Black male youth an "opportunity" to have crimes pinned on them when all other investigations fail. "Probably gang related."

Imagine urban American life offering young Black males the opportunity to fear gangs; gangs that could make them fear for their "air jump out of the gym" tennis shoes, even though they can't wear them if they're the wrong color; gangs that could make them fear for their dressed-out cars and low-rider trucks; gangs that could make them tremble in fear at the very word "carjacked;" carjacked to be used during the next drive-by, robbery, or joy ride and high-speed chase; gangs that could make them fear for their very lives here on earth. Membership or victim of membership both amount to winding up in some state's system of statistics, buried, or incarcerated at an early age.

Now, after we have imagined hundreds of years of slavery in which all traces of one's history has been removed, in which all respect and faith in one's parents has been systematically eliminated, in which the norm is the breakup of one's family (that would otherwise provide guidance and direction), we begin to come into focus.

After we have imagined one hundred and sixty years of past emancipation in which freedom for our youth means aimlessly seeking pursuits of happiness without direction, resources, self-respect, or respect for others, we have no choice but to imagine lawlessness and intent to do great bodily harm (all flowing from within our youth). For this imaginary scenario has said that all remnants of leadership, whether in the home or from within the Black community, has been met by a very consistent effort of "seek and destroy." Our imaginary present situation would show our youth as targets of unemployment, underemployment, prison systems, police suspicions, gang violence, concealed weapons laws, citizens watch groups, and finally victims of their own actions. Involvement in any wrongdoing is not a prerequisite. If we can imagine all this, let us imagine that our imagination is real. Then and only then can we begin to approach our Black male youth's present state of hopelessness and disarray.

SYMPTOMS OF DETERIORATION (REAL AND PERCEIVED)

If we are to address the issues that lead directly to failure and the seemingly hopeless state of our youth's future, we need to clearly identify them and then proceed further.

My list is by no means complete, and hopefully changes, extensions, updates, and corrections will be forthcoming from all sorts of critics. These I welcome as long as they are done from a functionally effective standpoint.

When I say symptoms of deterioration, real and perceived, I equate the two as equal. If there is a real problem, certainly it needs to be dealt with. It is a real problem, and it is perceived as real. If it is merely a perceived problem, having no basis in reality, it is still perceived as real and addressed accordingly. However, if it has no basis in reality, to address it as real is to address it in error. Allow me to repeat the last statement, for it is very critical in our youth's survival. "However, if it has no basis in reality, to address it as real is to address it in error." This is the area where we as parents make critical mistakes in rearing Black male youth. All is not as it seems, which is why we tend to falter.

My list of symptoms of deterioration is as follows:

- Failing grades
- Lack of confidence to achieve goals
- No direction for the future
- No respect for authority
- Hanging out with the wrong crowd
- Always late and other time factors
- Uncontrolled spending
- Wants everything given to them
- No integrity/no accountability
- Profane rap music
- Drug use or drug dealing

FAILING GRADES AND LACK OF CONFIDENCE TO ACTUALIZE THEIR HUMAN POTENTIAL: THE LEARNING EXPERIENCE

Failing in school and lack of self-determination to earn decent grades certainly leads our youth toward dropping out. At the very least, it internalizes an attitude of failure. Poor achievement in school could easily be a symptom of some other problem, such as problems at home, peer group influences, or a host of other detrimental ailments.

In this section, however, I will address the learning experience, beginning with the confidence factor. From there I will attempt to pick up on toddlers' learning experiences and work my way through the possibilities.

We see young Black male students receiving inferior grades that are often attributed to lack of confidence. If they are our youth, we should make attempts at building this confidence to a level that is at least acceptable for minimal achievement. Often we fail in this because we attempt to talk this confidence factor into their being. We treat confidence as if it is some sort of religious experience. "Believe in yourself and you can do anything," we say. Still nothing happens and the failures continue. Then we show them examples of other's achievements gained through confidence and yet it still does not seat. We constantly remind them that there is no success without confidence except through luck. It seems our youth are fresh out of luck, and we still can't get the confidence thing to sink in. Our task then is to get a handle on this mystic entity called confidence and somehow transpose it upon our youth's being.

First of all, confidence is not a mystic entity or even a psychological entity. It has its basis grounded in reality. It is merely one of the stages of success. Allow me to explain. All too often we as parents of Black males feel that we send them to school to learn all there is to learn. We even bus them, sending them to what we perceive to be the best public and private schools, and we rest assured that the learning experience will be completed. In essence, the learning experience comes from home and only the basics are taught in primary and secondary schools. These basics are taught to be accepted as truths. By the time they have graduated or dropped out, they've had numerous years of accepting basic truths, many of which we as parents hold. Yet, though educated to various degrees and accepting many of these truths, teens lose interest in furthering their education due to a lack of confidence and following their peers through all types of phases and fads. These two conditions greatly contribute to their present state of affairs, and they overshadow these basic truths. In the area of confidence, we parents have to separate the thought of learning those things necessary for our youth's survival from those things taught in the educational institutions. Certainly a sound formal education is necessary as a start, but it will not give our youth the confidence they need to succeed.

Confidence, we should know, is not a mystic entity falling from the heavens, landing on some people and completely missing others. Justifiable confidence is grounded in reality. Thus it is not just a state of mind. One can be a very mentally confident person and fail miserably. We see it every day when psychologically confident individuals open small businesses, only to later close, leaving behind mountains of debt and depleted savings accounts. This type of individual had determination, money, and perhaps good ideas. What he did not have was confidence that was grounded in reality.

Confidence that is grounded in reality comes only from experience. Experience comes only from repetition, repetition, and more repetition. Repetition comes from two sources: 1) from one's own individual actions and sightings, and 2) from the actions, sightings, and communication of others, such as through dialogue or reading. A couple of examples should clarify this point.

The first time a youth or anyone else studies a difficult topic, it will be just that. Difficult. After a second reading it will begin to sink in somewhat better. After a third reading the subject matter becomes even easier. If a fourth reading takes place, we feel very good about the upcoming examination.

What we have just done is repeatedly read the material. This gave us a measure of expertise on the subject matter, allowing us to feel very good about the examination. This is truly confidence grounded in reality, confidence that came from experience, which was derived from the repetition of reading the material four times. Once again, repetition gives experience, which gives confidence grounded in reality.

Example number two: The first time a kid, or anyone else for that matter, picks up a baseball bat, tennis racket, or basketball, his movements will be clumsy and uncoordinated. After repeated episodes in the sport, a measure of expertise develops. The more episodes encountered, the more his expertise develops. Eventually the movements become fluid and effective. The novice now feels good about himself in that particular sport. Once again, we have confidence that comes from experience that comes from repetition.

Confidence is part of a historical process leading up to greatness, which I will address later. Confidence is that part of a process by which one takes lack of skill (the past), works on achieving proficiency of the skill through repetition (also the past, but encompassing the present), and achieves the proficiency level known as experience (the present), culminating in a positive attitude to address the required task in the present and future.

As parents of Black males, it is our responsibility to teach them to achieve confidence. It will not be endowed upon them from the heavens, and it requires hard work, but it is achievable by all. Its components are basic—so basic that they can be applied to any endeavor, not just school.

School represents only the second phase of the learning process. Confidence in learning is enhanced or retarded long before the child enters formal educational institutions. As a matter of fact, this confidence in learning begins shortly after the newborn begins to visualize things in his initial environment.

Babies come into the world with only the instinctive behavior of sucking for sustenance. Before long, they begin to notice things around them. This is natural, but even more importantly, this is the point at which they begin to learn. This is also the point at which some of our most important work in their preparation for emancipated adulthood begins.

Being truly prepared for life is based on one's experiences. How we react to their natural learning behavior has a significant impact on that learning behavior. As the immobile infant gets more and more curious about his surroundings, we know that one day he will walk up to not just one item but all items to investigate. This is the first opportunity we will have to begin fulfilling our commitment to his learning process. This is also the beginning of many opportunities that we will have to build confidence in his learning behavior. If we buy into the theory that confidence comes only from experience and that experience comes only through repetition, why should the infant's confidence in learning have to wait until he is able to walk?

Take the immobile infant to those items of interest. We will know what is of interest to him because his eyes will focus on those items. Allow the infant to experience those items time and time again. Repetition. Make those items less of a curiosity. Harness and promote the learning process, especially during the child's immobile infancy. Do this regularly. An infant can do more than eat, pass waste, and cry. He can learn too, but only what we expose him to. If our job is to prepare children for adulthood, we've got a lot of work to do today.

We soon pass the stage of being parents to an immobile infant and our commitment grows even more. Perhaps tenfold. The previously immobile infant begins to walk, and the natural learning process is accelerated. The child wants to investigate everything, and we are going nuts. The child's mission in life is not to make our lives miserable but simply to learn. Take the time to show the child everything that captures his curiosity. If it is too dangerous, remove it. If it is too precious, lock it up in a vault. It shouldn't be out in the open anyway.

If we spank his hand for attempting to exhibit the learning process—that is, for getting into things—we are in essence spanking the learning process. If we repeatedly do this, we are showing the child that the learning experience is not OK. The confidence that should be blooming from experience through repetition has now turned into a lack of confidence because experience through repetition has shown that learning brings physical pain.

If we scold the child for wanting to learn about our "glass duck," we are again letting the child know that it displeases us for him to learn. Never underestimate the pain inflicted by the tongue. It is equally painful and can last a lot longer. However, if there is immediate danger involved such as light sockets, we have to do what we have to do, otherwise we may not get a second chance. (I can say don't spank the child's hand, but I can't say spank the child's hand, or spank the child, or even for us to scold the child. The child abuse people may interpret that as physical or psychological abuse. I personally think that allowing a child to electrocute himself is child abuse.) If you have stereos and other components of interest, teach the child to operate them properly. They will be less likely to destroy them if they know the operating procedures. Don't underestimate our children's ability to learn, and don't underestimate our ability to stifle that learning. Don't underestimate our ability to build a lack of confidence through negative experiences and repetition. We must always foster an environment conducive to building confidence in learning. Our youth will learn for the rest of their lives, and it will only get easier with our commitment and assistance. Our commitment to our youth's learning process is the first prerequisite for guaranteeing that they will have the confidence necessary to actualize their human potential.

What potential? Human potential. The potential that differentiates humans from other species. The potential that caused the ancients to build great civilizations. The human element in our being, all our beings, that has characteristics that allow us to be inventors and scholars.

Human beings are the only non-instinctive architects and philosophers. We erect monumental skyscrapers and underground sewage systems large and sophisticated enough to handle wastes of entire cities. Humans build flying machines that leave the spacious skies to travel in areas where there is no air. Humans conceive great democracies and republics that debate issues of freedom, abortion, and future generations.

Human potential is not some abstract theory whose existence is to be debated. Human potential simply "is." I'll leave whether it came as a religious gift or an evolutionary effect for the theologians and scholars to debate. But by virtue of their debate they acknowledge its existence. To deny its existence is to deny all creations, inventions, concepts, and realities associated with mankind's achievements over time.

To block or hinder all avenues of actualizing one's human potential is to reduce one to an animal-like state capable only of feeding, reproducing, and perhaps instinctively seeking shelter. To block or hinder all avenues of actualizing one's human potential without removing today's middle class standards of success is to invite theft, crime, and violence; theft and violence generated by a feeling of hopelessness; hopelessness casted by serious doubt of legitimate success; doubt generated by bleak futures and worthless educations. This is the state of hopelessness which reduces our black male youth to that animal-like state, to that hole that they have no hope of ever climbing out of.

We have to prepare them for their futures, but we can ill afford to prepare them for limited success. We must prepare them for unlimited success, and we can only do this by helping them realize and then acknowledge their humanity. We must explain to them that their humanity comes with a piece of standard equipment called "human potential," which is directly transferable into unlimited potential for success.

We must explain to our Black male youth that those who built the ancient civilizations, those who generated inventions that made us mobile, those that gave us light after sunset, were merely human. We must explain to them that those who generated great works of art, televisions, video games, and computers were merely human beings. What makes them great is that they actualized their human potential. They believed in their human potential. They had confidence that was grounded in reality through experience, which traveled the route of repetition.

They would not accept failure, for they knew that if they tried enough times and gained enough experience, they would eventually break through. There was no excuse big enough to cause them to fail, for they knew that failure in and of itself does not exist. They knew that failure was just another term for lack of experience, lack of repetition. When faced with a possible failure, one that understands his human potential merely goes back and adds to his arsenal of experience by stacking up the repetition. They did, however, know that if there was one thing that would cause failure and bring their actualizing of human potential to a screeching halt, it was the "legitimate excuse." The legitimate excuse is the deadliest of all obstacles obscuring the actualization of human potential. It has direct, immediate, and everlasting negative consequences on human potential.

The legitimate excuse causes the committed to prolong and procrastinate. It causes the motivated to quit. It causes human potential to lie down and go to sleep, waiting for a better day, which never comes. It causes one to sleep past all due dates, waking up in the past tense and in last place, a loser. The legitimate excuse gives concrete reasons for our Black male youth to push drugs. And what could be more concrete than fancy cars and the seemingly good life, when we all know that corporate America has put meaningful employment outside their grasp? The legitimate excuse is so deadly that it frequently shows future prospects so disheartening that it justifies suicide. We parents of Black male youth must confer upon them the dangers that accompany the legitimate excuse. We must warn them of its sorcery. We must show them its impact on their human potential, which is otherwise a given. It is the only given that promotes healthy future generations of prosperity and greatness. To talk about greatness in our youth would be meaningless unless there is a clear picture of what constitutes it. All of those that we see it in are no different than you, me, or our youth. What makes them appear great is the historical process that they progressed through. They merely took some past body of knowledge or skill, practiced it to proficiency, learned all they needed to know about it, and combined it with some other previous body of knowledge. This union of previously separated disciplines now creates a new discipline, one on a different level. Allow me a couple of examples.

A chemist takes some acids that he knows the properties of and puts them in a container that the acids won't eat up. He takes his metallurgy experience and decides to add lead plates. This simple combination results in the storage batteries that start most of the modern world's automobiles.

The storage batteries would certainly qualify as a great invention. Though my example may seem like a simplistic instance of greatness, it is not. The only thing that has been downplayed is the repetition required in acquiring his experience in chemistry, plastics, and metallurgy. The end result is the same: a great invention. Let me try another example.

A teen of average size finds himself being bullied daily. At his wits' end, he decides to try and put a stop to the bullying and joins a health club. Upon joining, he sees himself for what he really is: a ninety-eight-pound weakling like me. He decides not only to stop the bullying, but to also transform his puny body into one of massive muscles. Only through direct repetition of pumping iron could this be achieved. He commits, and he pumps iron. He pumps iron and commits to more iron pumping, and he pumps and he pumps and he pumps. He physically begins to develop, and he pumps even more iron. With the physical development gained through commitment and repetition, those he previously thought were built now begin to marvel at him. They talk him into entering contests, and he begins to win. Now he's winning and pumping iron. Pretty soon, he wins the ultimate contest: Mr. Cosmos. Being on the weight-lifting circuit takes him out of the bullied environment, but one day while not touring, he runs into the bully. Guess what? NO MORE BULLY.

Though my examples are simplified and silly, the essence of greatness still remains. And once again it is comprised of repetition, experience, and confidence (grounded in reality), which is magnified into different levels (of greatness) based on one's commitment.

As with anything else that evolves, the entire scenario of one individual's greatness is merely one of many historical cycles. In both of my examples, nothing new was generated. They were merely new combinations of things and processes generated through the actualization of human potential. To rob our youth of this realization is to doom them to their present state of hopelessness for generations to come. To acknowledge their humanity and human potential is to give their greatness a chance to come forward. It is our parental duty to make sure they see these concepts work and to make sure they understand the entire process. With all the modern-day confusion and distractions, they cannot perceive their potential for greatness, and it seems that we've forgotten to tell them about it. Many of us didn't know that it existed within ourselves. Believe in our youth. They are the greats of tomorrow, for if it is not in them, there will be none.

The previously mentioned concepts are most certainly applicable to the formal education process, which is our youth's primary job if they are to be prepared for tomorrow's realities. In keeping with this theme, we, not our youth's teachers, have to be in charge of the overall educational process (note how the word "process" keeps popping up). This is especially true with all the constraints placed on today's teachers by law enforcement officials and child experts.

The educational institutions, as I mentioned earlier, provide merely the basics in the primary and secondary grades. They put the material out there and then it is up to the child's study discipline to determine whether it is digested. This study discipline can only come from home when we are dealing with overcrowded schools and understaffed, underpaid, handcuffed teachers.

As our commitment once again comes to the forefront, let us assume a youth is not doing well in school. In order to get him back on a winning educational track, we must first bypass his grades. They are actually the least of our worries since we already know what is required for him to excel. (Hint: repetition, experience, confidence.) Examine the child. Is there a learning disability? I mean a real disability and not some label placed on him because of an impatient, inept educational system trying to get more state aid with the help of equally inept psychological professionals. If so, the youth will be doing poorly in all classes related to the disability. Vision and hearing problems as well as other real disabilities require professional help.

If there are no real disabilities, ask his peers and teachers some basic questions. How do the other kids view him? How does he view himself? What are his strengths? What are his weaknesses? How is his attendance? (Don't ever assume you know this.) How is his timeliness on in-school assignments? How is his timeliness on homework assignments? Are there errors due to carelessness? Does he have trouble comprehending the material? Ask these questions and any others that are pertinent to the youth's educational well-being.

Once these questions are answered, we can begin to work on an educational process designed to give our youth the confidence (grounded in reality through repetition and experience) necessary to guarantee good grades. Study time should be constant and every day (except weekends, which I will address shortly). For instance, have him study two hours per day. This should not be based on completion of the homework assignment. If completion of an assignment takes more than the prescribed study time, then so be it. If it takes less time, then have the youth read for the duration. Get him used to longer-term study periods. High school and most certainly college could easily require more time just to get by. He will need the discipline. Have him read ahead. Remember, the youth is behind. Have him read materials outside of the school curriculum.

If he doesn't have his own reading interests, choose some for him, but above all, have him read.

I mentioned earlier that there should be no homework on the weekends. This has its own benefits. As the job is to prepare him for adult life, consider that we don't like to work on weekends. Neither does he. The weekend is for recuperation. Let him relax. In addition to recuperation, if the home rules dictate absolutely no weekend homework, we have eliminated Sunday night cramming, a very bad habit. Also, no weekend homework frees up his weekend to assist in the accountability process, which I will get to shortly.

If he is having trouble comprehending the material, it could be due to an underdeveloped vocabulary. Have him use the dictionary. It will take him about two years of looking up every word he doesn't understand to build a decent comprehensive vocabulary. Comprehension building is another aspect of the confidence-building process. Looking up every word (repetition) will most certainly give him the experience to exhibit confidence in both his speaking and writing abilities. Have the youth apply this same type of consistency to math, science, and anything else he is involved in, with the understanding that all learning is a process. The word process keeps coming up. Allow me to explain the functional significance of the process concept. It is also grounded in reality.

Success is not the result of the finished product. Success is the result of the process that goes into creating the finished product. Failure is not the result of the end product. Failure is the result of the process that goes or does not go into the end product. Therefore, both success and failure are the products of the processes that go into them.

For instance, the examination is not passed or failed when it is graded. The examination is passed or failed during the preparation or lack thereof. A basketball game is not won or lost at game time. It is won or lost in preparation for the game. Our Black male youth's future is not successful or unsuccessful when they turn twenty-one. Their success or failure is determined by the preparatory process they've been through or haven't been through. This process can only be guided by our commitment to them and that process. Our commitment, which is also a process, is the only process by which we can ensure their success.

Let us assume your youth or mine is the instigator of an occasional classroom infraction. He blurts out loud, talks back to the teacher, and otherwise disrupts the class. This is the opportunity for us to teach him accountability. As I stated earlier, there has evolved an enormous social climate to make the Black male youth accountable for his actions. Those Black male youth that are not taught accountability at home will be taught it through more and more prisons, certification of youth as adults, and supporting legislation authorizing the "good citizens" to carry concealed weapons (for protection of course). The difference is that this type of accountability has no regard for their future, learning experience, or even their lives.

By reserving weekends for recreational activities, we have already created the time through which to hold him accountable for his actions. As an example, my child initiates a classroom infraction. Each infraction costs him two hours of weekend time plus the time it takes me to straighten things out. If I have to take off from work for three hours to correct this situation, he owes me five hours of weekend time: two for the infraction and three for my time lost. This amounts to five hours of weekend household maintenance.

I'll let you in on a little secret. He will soon learn that he values not just his time, but also my time and the teacher's. If you think this is harsh, ask yourself what else the teacher could do besides inform us. And why should we lose three hours' pay with nothing gained? We didn't disrupt the class. Five hours of household maintenance is a small price for him to pay versus five years of confinement and labor for one small infraction with the law. It is one and the same. Teaching accountability then is a process. It is the only process through which we can have confidence in our youth's conduct. That confidence absolutely has to be grounded in the realities of the experiences of his being held accountable for each and every repetitious act of misconduct.

DIRECTION FOR THE FUTURE

Our Black male youth are faced with so much uncertainty and despair for the future that their only positive outlook is in their dreams. And yet their dreams, and even ours, are some of the most misunderstood elements that we come into contact with. If they even dream at all, they dream of becoming professional ball players, artists, architects, doctors, lawyers, and rich and famous movie stars. Their aspirations tend to be quite a bit beyond the clouds.

Parents, being of a more practical nature, advise them to get a decent education and to pursue a more obtainable job. We often, in our infinite wisdom, suggest that they stop dreaming and get down to business, that they get more in touch with reality, that they prepare themselves for a real job in a major corporation. Let us take a brief look at these real jobs.

In the days of old, this country evolved through an industrial revolution creating assembly lines that dramatically increased production and thus the need for labor. There was a drastic increase in the need for mining products, foundry products, manufactured items, subassembly items, final assembly products, marketing, and finally sales. Once inventories dropped to certain levels in relation to sales, the entire process started over again and economic growth continued. This cycle was only interrupted when inflation was deemed out of control, which then required adjustments in interest rates. If interest rates were handled properly, which usually didn't happen, the country avoided a recession and the economic growth continued. Prosperity was at least within our reach once the legislature said that so many Blacks had to be allowed to work. Smokestack industries were in abundance. Then, out of "economic necessity," many large corporations began outsourcing the work to foreign countries where labor costs were often cheaper. Company profits continued to soar, but only if one could "sell himself" to a prospective employer did he have a fighting chance for meaningful employment. In the meantime, major corporations continuously reduced their ranks.

Since labor-driven products were being reduced through outsourcing and labor-saving devices called robotics, new companies began to focus on service-oriented products such as the ordering and delivery of goods that used to be made in this country.

With the advent of the computer age, further downsizing continued, but this time it even extended to the service sector. You pick up the telephone, dial your number, listen to a computer message, press another number, listen to another message, and then press another number. If you press enough numbers and listen to enough messages, you might get to talk to a human. Every number that you press represents at least one displaced job.

This downsizing effort has continued into at least its fourth decade. Downsizing now continues regardless of the state of the national economy or the economic health of its individual companies. The days of being able to say that there have been five continuous generations of Browns working at XYZ company are over (unless you happen to be the grandson of Mr. XYZ).

We have to seriously question giving our Black male youth directions to place their primary focus for employment in corporate America. It will only lead to their disappointment and frustration as it has led to ours. What then, if anything, should be their primary focus for the future? It seems that when the economy is growing too fast due to the spending of money, this inflationary factor comes from those companies that are growing in size and in employment. If the major corporations are downsizing (as they have been on a constant basis for the past four decades), this growth then has to be coming from small businesses. It would then necessarily follow that this is where the new jobs are being created. If this is true, it would explain why the Small Business Administration has always survived congressional tampering. And the Small Business Administration focuses its efforts on companies that create not major products and services but many minor products and services. These minor products and services, not being the products of major corporations, are the end result of small businesses, even more so of the entrepreneurial spirit: someone's dream.

They are the products and services of an individual that dared to take focus away from corporate America. They are the efforts of someone that dared to try and try again (repetition) until they built enough experience to give them the confidence to achieve their measure of greatness. This greatness manifests itself in an actualized dream. This greatness manifests itself in self-sufficiency. This greatness manifests itself sometimes in wealth but always in self-confidence, self-fulfillment, self-worth, and at the least a very strong feeling of accomplishment.

All this stems from actualized dreams. More importantly, self-confidence, self-fulfillment, self-sufficiency, and self-worth are the direct antithesis of our youth's present state of affairs, the animal-like state created by a justifiable perception of hopelessness. The key word in all of this is dreams. Dreams, it appears, represent the only reality for tomorrow. They are the only opportunities for tomorrow. If we are to prepare our Black male youth for the realities of tomorrow, not only must we allow them to dream and aspire, but we must also foster, promote, and support their dreams today. In their preparation for tomorrow, the dream becomes primary and the preparation for a job in a quickly dwindling job market becomes secondary. Times have changed, and if our youth are to be in sync with this change, we absolutely must communicate to them that tomorrow's reality is today's dream, and yesterday's reality (a corporate career) is but a daydream. Start them off on a path toward actualizing their dreams instead of impeding them, for to destroy their dreams is to destroy their future.

RESPECTING AUTHORITY

In addressing the question of respect for authority, we must be clear on three things: (1) What is not authority? (2) What is authority? And (3) Why should our youth respect authority?

(1) By authority, I do not mean adults, policemen, other law officials, teachers, or the entire blanket conceptions of authority figures. We have seen the above-mentioned list commit crimes that totally baffle the imagination. As such we cannot give them a universal seal of approval simply because they hold their positions. To do so would be extremely shallow. However, we must still reserve judgment on this group based on factors to be addressed shortly. (2) What is authority? Authority is the ability or received delegation of the ability to give and enforce initiatives upon others. Authority is the controlling entity of the endeavor one is involved with. The previously mentioned list of authority figures should always fall under this definition. Often they do not because of their involvement in acts outside of their designated assignments. (3) Why should our Black male youth respect authority, or should they? This question is answered based on the overall objective for involvement in the endeavor.

Any endeavor our youth (or even ourselves) are involved in is entered into in anticipation of a certain measure of success. We don't embark on tasks seeking failure. No society and no group of people on earth have ever had an ambition to fail. Successful completion of the task then is the objective. Otherwise, why waste the time and energy?

If good grades are the overall objective, one must respect the teacher, for the teacher is the controlling entity presiding over grades. Disrespecting the teacher, whether a good teacher or a bad teacher, makes failure imminent. Disrespecting the teacher, and failing because of it, violates the original goal, which was to achieve a passing grade. Issuing a failing grade is the teacher's way of holding our youth accountable for their disrespectful ways. If the objective of our youth is driving from point A to point B, speeding up and down the street is disrespecting the traffic laws. Disrespecting the traffic laws signals the police. The policeman will pull over our youth to ticket them, consuming their time by detaining them and making tardiness eminent. This is not in line with the original intent of our youth, which was to get to point A from point B. The police officer is the controlling entity that presides over the traffic laws. Giving our youth speeding tickets, which also have to be paid for years to come through rising insurance rates, is the policeman's way of holding our youth accountable for their disrespectful ways. Even if our youth are involved in gangs or selling drugs, there is a controlling entity. Disrespecting the authority of the gang or drug scene makes death imminent. Killing our Black male youth for disrespecting gang or drug scene authority is the gang leader or drug kingpin's way of holding our youth accountable for their disrespectful ways.

The intention is not to make spineless cowards out of our youth (none of us could do that anyway, regardless of how hard we try). The intention is not to imply that authority is not to be challenged, especially since authority figures as a group don't seem to have the world's greatest ethics. The intention is not even to say that rules are not to be broken, especially when many of the rules are unfair and unjust to our Black male youth, such as a perpetual "Bill of Rights" for "true Americans" and "affirmative action" for our youth that is subject to reevaluation every so often. The intention, however, is to have them always bear in the forefront of their minds that the presiding authority, whether legal, illegal, aboveboard, or shady, is not about to lie down and crumble in the face of any half-concerted effort of disrespect on their parts. As a matter of fact, authority figures expect challenges. This gives them the opportunity to reassert themselves as that authority. They reassert themselves by making examples of our youth through the process of accountability. If our youth are going to disrespect authority by breaking rules, disrupting classes, and not fulfilling their academic requirements, they'd better be willing to make the long-term commitment to ensure the successfulness of their disrespectful ways. They'd better take a minute to examine whether or not speeding up and down the street or not completing a class project efficiently and on time is worth the long-term commitment required to disrespect the controlling entity. Most importantly they'd better know whether the long-term commitment to rule violations is in line with the overall objective. If it is not, they have created an obstacle that must be overcome simply to get back to the starting gate.

Most often our youth's commitment to acts of disrespecting authority is short termed. They are often seeking a short-term thrill, trying to make a point to peers that five years down the line will be meaningless or detrimental to their long-term well-being, or even simply doing as others do and not having a conscious motive. Those that are in authority usually have a lifelong commitment to keeping that authority. Teachers enter teaching as a career choice. Police officers enter law enforcement as a career choice. Drug dealers enter drug dealing as a career choice. Gang leaders are equally committed to their roles of leadership.

The weights that are supposed to balance the scales are of uneven magnitudes. Our youth have short-term commitments to acts of disrespect and the presiding authorities are committed for life, thus making our youth's failure imminent. Our job once again is to prepare and train our youth for emancipation. One of life's lessons is the understanding of how authority figures respond to challenges as well as their commitments to retaining those positions of authority. To not communicate these realities to our youth is equivalent to disarming them and then sending them out to do battle with an armed adversary. It is equivalent to entrapment. It is equivalent to ambushing our own youth. It is equivalent to imminent failure. It could well be equivalent to imminent death or incarceration. Teach them the rules of how authority works. Their very lives may depend on this understanding.

SIGNIFICANT OTHERS AND HANGING OUT WITH THE WRONG CROWD

Our youth's study discipline as well as their discipline toward success in any endeavor is often a reflection of our discipline toward the completion of projects. They mimic what they are shown, for their limited exposure in life awards them few original concepts, creations, and outlooks.

If we buy that repetition and experience guides the way to confidence, we know that our unsuccessful completion of any project is unacceptable. This makes the risk/reward ratio in accepting the commitment to any project suspect. The projects that we parents take on may seem admirable in the beginning, but all too often they wind up being overwhelming. This is one of the reasons why we must be extremely critical of the tasks we undertake. Certainly we can deal with an occasional failure, quitting because the rewards of success do not merit the commitment.

But can our Black male youth accept the idea of our unexplained failure? Can they afford to see us as mortal and fragile, capable of all the shortcomings associated with mortality, including inconsistency and failure? I think not. If failure after failure becomes acceptable to us, their heroes, their epitome of strength, knowledge, and wisdom, then failure becomes acceptable to them, for they are the reflection of all that we have taught them, good, bad, or indifferent. They are the reflection of our persistence and determination, or they become the mirror images of our failures. They must grow up thinking, knowing, and believing that we, their parents, cannot conceive of failure and that all insurmountable odds are merely legitimate excuses that will eventually be overcome through repetition and experience. They must grow up knowing that hell will freeze over, thaw, and freeze over again before we will give up on any project, for this is part of our commitment to them. Then and only then will they grow up with the same persistence and determination to succeed in all their endeavors. We must be selective in the tasks we choose to make a priority. For our youth to witness our failures on a repetitive basis is to give them negative experiences of us to internalize, for we are their significant others.

"Significant others" is a sociological term simply meaning significant other person or persons. As I stated earlier, we parents of Black male youth begin their educational process. We allow them to experience our precious "glass ducks," and we teach them that both fire and the kitchen stove are hot. We teach them how to operate the computer. As I stated earlier, our youth see us not only as the total epitome of knowledge, but more importantly, the sole source of all they have learned. We have become their significant other. This position must never be compromised.

But we do compromise this position. The things that we do directly affect their behavior, for it is our teachings that they learn. With or without conscious intent we teach them that it is alright for their mother or father to stay out till dawn. We teach them that wives should be beaten and that it is alright to speed up and down the street while driving. We teach them that it is alright for adults to argue or to not go to work. We teach them that it is alright to quit in the middle of a project. We even teach them the vulgarities that we object to in their music. Our youth have invented or created next to nothing. All that they do—the good, the bad, and the ugly—they have learned from us.

I cannot overemphasize the importance of the position that we hold. Throughout their emancipation, we have to watch everything that we do or say. They believe our ways of doing things are how they should be done, and I guarantee that they will act accordingly. We must act as we would have them act. This is not a matter of choice. Their very survival depends on it. Committed or not, we are their significant others.

When we are wrong in our judgment and behavior, and from time to time we will be, we must immediately own up to our errors. If we don't, our youth will eventually find out anyway. For them to find out that we were in error and tried to just let it pass or tried to conceal it is equivalent to lying to them. Our youth will not tolerate a verbal lie or the living of a lie from their significant others. They will respond inwardly first and begin to view us as plain mortal beings subject to the frailties of lying, deceit, or worse. They will distrust us and make evaluations on our comments, actions, and judgments. This state of mind in our youth makes it difficult if not impossible to teach them even the barest of necessities for their successful survival in urban America. At that point they must find a new significant other. They must find a new source of strength. They must find a new source of knowledge. Through repetition and experience we have destroyed their confidence in us. Because they relied on us for their inner strength, we have created the type of faulty situation that causes them to yield to peer pressure, for that missing inner strength must be replaced. We may have also created the conditions necessary for them to seek refuge in gang membership. We cannot afford to give them verbal lies or to live lies, for our youth are seeking answers and will find them elsewhere if ours are unacceptable, suspect, or untrustworthy.

They will find answers that are flawed but acceptable to them. They will find answers that are stifling but acceptable to them. They will eventually find answers that are deadly but acceptable to them. These answers may well be found in the gurus perpetuating drug use, drug dealing, gang membership, and gang-related activities that may include murder. The new answers found could easily lead to their lives being wasted, incarcerated, or taken. As I stated earlier, the position of significant other is never to be compromised. Its primary function is to teach. Did we teach our Black male youth that they can always trust our words and that our words are equaled only by our actions and judgment? Did we teach them that we will always own up to our errors? Did we teach them that our commitment to them is first and foremost and that this commitment to them causes us to place our selfish ways on the back burner? Our youth's trust and confidence in our abilities to teach them life is the only defense that we can ever have to guard them from the unacceptable answers and misguided directions offered to them by hanging out with the wrong crowd.

TIME

Late to bed, late to rise, running wild trying to get there. Late for school, late for work, and in a mad frenzy when our youth should be comfortably contemplating their next move. Driving fast, getting tickets and higher insurance rates. Running, simply in a hurry, only to be viewed by passing police cars and deemed a suspect. Late in life: By the time they've figured out that they need a job, all the good ones are gone. By the time they've figured out that they need an education, they are no longer young. By the time they have figured out time, they're wise enough to come in last.

Giving our youth a sense of timeliness is perhaps a very difficult task due to our own adopted sense of timeliness. We will not be able to teach our youth one thing if we exhibit to them that it is really done a different way. They will not subscribe to the "do as I say, not as I do" philosophy. They will always pick up on what we've shown them, for we are their significant others.

When we speed in our cars, we can rest assured that they will speed in theirs. We act as if we're barely making our deadlines, and we probably are. We push through traffic, weaving in and out, having accidents that ultimately make us either late or absent from our destinations. We push to finish deadlines at the last minute, and it shows up in the quality of the work performed. We even rush to get to entertainment activities. Afterward, we rush to get home to relax. When we get through rushing, at best we have only arrived there on time. What an adrenaline flow. No wonder all the hypertension and high blood pressure.

Before we can teach our youth timeliness, we have to learn it ourselves. We must stop tolerating last-minute requests from both friends and relatives unless it is absolutely necessary. We must teach our youth, friends, and other relatives that adequate time is a must for all endeavors except emergencies. When we start early, we teach our youth to start early. Teach them, by example of course, to get up early enough to not have to rush to school. When we teach them to get an early start on homework assignments, we teach them to get an early start on life.

Besides, no one's work is at its best when it's been rushed through. Haste does indeed make waste. Teaching them that it's alright to rush is equivalent to teaching them habits of carelessness. Teach them that all their work should be done in an atmosphere of relaxation, which can only come from allowing sufficient time to complete the objective.

One way of assuring an atmosphere of relaxation is by monitoring their time. By monitoring their time, I don't mean making them feel as if they're under a magnifying glass. However, just as they know our whereabouts at all times, in case of an emergency or just a simple need, we should know theirs. They know where we are, and we don't feel watched. That same necessity belongs to us if we are to build a sense of timeliness in them.

Our youth have so much morning time for hygiene, breakfast, and travel to school; so much time for school; so much time for athletics (if involved); so much time for chores, recreation, and dinner; and so much time for homework, hygiene, and sleep (not necessarily in that order). Violating any one of these time factors will be at the expense of the others. All are necessary if our youth are simply to get through tomorrow in a relaxed manner.

Late night running is not conducive to being prepared in this cruel and unforgiving world. Oversleep and their grades suffer. Oversleep and their jobs suffer. It is one and the same. Train them to be responsive to their own time requirements. The system already monitors their time, as is evidenced by the many municipalities that have evoked teen curfews. Violating these curfews comes with minor sanctions. Nevertheless, we are trying to get away from our youth enduring sanctions by the system. We are most certainly trying to get away from allowing the system to train our youth, for it is the same system that has created or allowed the creation of the bleak outlook that they have for their futures. It is the same system that will pick them up for curfew violation or suspicion and lock them up with those that have given up on the system. Locking them up for curfew violations with "criminal elements" may seem like an extreme case of monitoring their time, but I assure you it is not. Ask any group of ten Black male inner-city youth about being locked up with "real criminals" and then ask yourself if this is an extreme example. Monitor their time to allow them to successfully complete the educational process. Monitor their time so that the educational process is completed in an atmosphere of relaxation. Monitor their time so that they won't be late later on in life. Monitor their time now or else others will.

GIVING OUR BLACK MALE YOUTH A HISTORICAL OUTLOOK

It is truly amazing how we've studied massive amounts of history in formalized educational institutions and yet do not have a single clue as to history's impact on our futures. Our Black male youth have endured much of the same, and they've gotten about as much out of it as we have. We've both studied European history, African history, American history, African American history, the history of this and the history of that. At best, our youth have been culturally enlightened, but cultural enlightenment will not strengthen their perspectives on the future. They absolutely must have a historical outlook. I've written earlier that this or that was a historical process. We've maybe heard others say that "those who do not heed history's warnings are doomed to repeat it." Certainly we've all heard that "what goes around comes around." Allow me to attempt some clarity from a practical standpoint.

History is merely the past: good, bad, or indifferent. However, it is not just lying there in isolation unattached to its own past or its future as if flat. It has more of a spiral nature. It gives a deceptive circular appearance, in that historical events always seem to end up where they started. Allow me some examples.

You get up, go to work, go to bed, and then start it all over again. This gives the appearance of one total day of history. Winter comes, then spring, summer, and fall, only to start with winter all over again. Economic growth, rising interest rates, economic slowdowns, layoffs, recessions, and the lowering of interest rates equals one economic revolution that starts economic growth again. We buy a new car, it ages, becomes a problem, and then it's time to buy a new car again. The rich send their kids to the best schools. They get the best educations, then the best positions in life, only to start the process over again by sending their kids to the best schools.

Viewing these revolutions as circular and inevitable is what gives history its deceptive character. All these circular-looking events can be altered, which makes an understanding of history to the benefit of the Black male youth. To get up day in and day out without making daily preparations to get out of a dead-end job is to acknowledge and accept history's deceptive circular character. To make daily preparations to actualize one's dreams and aspirations is to assure that they are the future's reality. To go through high utility bills in the summer and winter and overpriced winter coats on an annual basis is to acknowledge and accept history's deceptive circular character. To insulate one's house in the spring or fall and to purchase winter coats during the summer is to reduce temperature comfort costs. To become the victim of the economic downturns repeatedly and without making preparations is to ensure that you will be its victim. To wait for the upcoming recession fully prepared is to purchase that expensive dream house at a rock-bottom price. To save for our youth's education, starting during his infancy is to send him to the best school eighteen years later.

In all actuality, history is not circular and events never return to their exact origin. Even the annual changes in seasons are not circular, for if they were, we could predict the exact temperature for every single day of the year. Even the meteorologists cannot do that. It will either be warmer or cooler, but not the same as a year ago.

History has a definite spiral nature. Each and every time (just like going around a gigantic coil spring) that we return to what we consider to be the front, we will either be at a higher level or a lower level, but never at the same level.

Each and every time we go through history's revolutions, we have either advanced upward or descended downward. If we have not learned from the downward steps, we are doomed to repeat the process, crossing over those same spiral steps in our quest to reach the top. If our youth have not been taught to view history (which is made each and every day of their lives) in the reality of its spiral nature, they have no choice but to cross over these same spiral revolutions. These spiral revolutions are what I term the historical experience. Historical experience applies to me, you, all our friends and relatives, and even the adversaries of our youth's futures. Most importantly it applies to our youth. What they don't know will most certainly hurt them. It is our duty to make sure they understand, forever and always, that the future is impacted by the process of historical experience, that historical experience (or any type of experience for that matter) is comprised of the events that make up that experience (which is repetition).

To impart this upon our youth is to give them a head start in life, for with this understanding there will be no more failures. What is now considered a failure will be put in its proper perspective. Failure will be considered a lack of historical experience. Failure will be considered a lack of emphasis placed on the process involved in completing the endeavor. With this comes the understanding that success or failure never rests in the final results but in the historical process leading up to the final results. This is what will mandate proper preparation for their endeavors. The understanding of the historical perspective is what will cause us to commit to their futures, and whether I am right or completely wrong, it is my perception of history that caused me to commit to this book, which is my contribution to their futures. Let us not make our youth repeat history. To give them a historical outlook is to dissolve the outlook of hopelessness and makes them know what they have to do. To not give them a historical perspective is to send them out aimlessly into the world to stumble over previously crossed paths. This would certainly be a wasteful use of both their time and their lives. It would also be wasteful of ours, for we are all that they will ever have to fall back on. Equip them to always have one watchful eye stacking up experience for their future and the other eye watching what they do today. If we can accomplish this, they will never get stuck repeating the past. Nevertheless, the world moves on, whether they see its realities or not.

GIVING THEM THE THINGS WE NEVER HAD

Making sure our youth are not denied the pleasures that we were denied is one of the most serious practices that we engage in. It contributes chronically to our present dilemma. It is misunderstood, and as with any tool, if not handled properly, it becomes a deadly weapon in the wrong hands. This "giving" has far-ranging consequences for both our youth themselves and the community at large.

Outside of the basic necessities of food, clothing and shelter, gifts and presents that are extra, whether we know it or not, represents additional learning experiences for our youth. Freedoms to do this or freedoms to do that represent similar learning experiences. When we raise our youth with gifts, money (outside of their basic allowances, if given) and freedom to roam simply because they exist, they acknowledge this easily and it becomes accepted as both fitting and proper. After years of repetition, these experiences make them confident that this is the way life is.

By exhibiting to them that they get simply because they exist, we have actually taught them (through repetition) that the world owes them something. You and I know that this is contrary to reality, yet we have taught them this behavior. This is in direct conflict with our goals, which is to prepare them for the realities of tomorrow. Anything learned that is not correct will have to be unlearned before one can go forward. In this particular case, we have caused our youth to take at least one step backward. Learning that they don't get things simply because they exist has to be quite painful, for in the future, reality will interfere with the way they were raised. In addition to this, they will also have to learn that they must work for the things they want. This is a one-hundred-and-eighty-degree turn. They have been pointed in exactly the wrong direction. Reality says that when we want extra money, we must work overtime. The boss does not shower us with the extra money simply because we exist. We must earn the extra money. This is what we must teach our youth. Let us not detach them from reality. When we make outstanding contributions at work, if we are nonunion employees, we may receive bonuses. We don't receive them each and every time we exhibit excellence in our jobs, but at least we've increased the opportunities. Even if we are hourly union employees, when we show extra initiative by working extra hours, we receive extra pay. When our youth exhibit extra initiative, we can use this as an opportunity to give them the extras, for they have earned them. We do not want to give them the extras first and then hope that they will do what is required, all the while hoping that they will turn out alright. How can they? We have pointed them in the wrong direction.

If we think this is the worst-case scenario, prepare for more. Yes, it gets even more detrimental. Our youth asks us for things and freedoms and sometimes we say no for whatever reason. They insist and we still say no. They continue to insist and then we give in. We say yes, maybe because when we were kids we always wanted one of those or wanted to do that. "What's the big deal?" we say. Why not let them enjoy their youth? What harm can it do?

It is not that simple, for we have just taught them that they can extract things from us that we originally were not willing to give. Their insistence boils down to their will versus ours. We are supposed to be the parents and yet they have extracted something from us against our original will without giving anything in return.

When this type of situation occurs over and over again through repetition, their experiences give them the confidence to attempt this on nonfamily members. When these nonfamily members resist, as in the past, it becomes a contest of will. When this is done with total strangers, it is called armed robbery. Let me repeat!! When this is done with total strangers, it is called armed robbery.

Our giving things does not prepare them for reality, and our giving in to their beckoning teaches them that by insisting, they can get things that others do not wish to give. This behavior is certainly not in line with our objectives. We have not even begun to approach anything close to a work ethic.

Instead, we have handicapped them. This behavior, receiving things simply because they exist or because they insist on having them, will eventually have to be unlearned. Unlearning the wrong way of doing anything and then learning the proper way of doing things is equivalent to repeating history before one can go forward. We have handicapped them in the sense that, as they go up and down history's revolving spiral, the rest of the world goes forward. When we give because they exist, we have given all of those that are in touch with reality a head start on the Black male youth. When compounded with historical injustices as well as present assaults on them (anti-affirmative action movements, anti-minimum wage increase movements, more and more prisons for them, concealed weapons legislation), any step backward puts them in direct visual contact with that state of hopelessness that can only result in the uncontrolled behavior that our youth exhibit. They have neither the time nor the patience to unlearn faulty lessons that we might teach. Do not love our youth to the point of helplessness. Do not love our youth to the point of hopelessness. Instead, teach them (by repetition of course) that rewards come from work. Teach them to appreciate the fruits of their labor. Instead of giving them the trinkets we never had, let's give them the things that we should have had and that they so dearly need now. Let's give them caring parents committed to their guidance. Let's give them caring parents committed to their integrity, for to be able to appreciate the fruits of their labor is truly for them to have learned integrity. Give them a chance to live a productive and unselfish life. Most importantly, let's allow them to live with a realistic assessment of adulthood.

INTEGRITY

Integrity: being of sound principles that are actualized in all of one's actions.

This is another one of those very delicate topics—not delicate in the sense of being philosophically sophisticated, but delicate in the sense of establishing parameters for our Black male youth to stay within.

Integrity, like confidence, is also not a mystic entity falling from the heavens, endowing itself on some and missing others completely. It is learned behavior. It is learned righteousness. It is learned honesty and learned sincerity. In order to teach righteousness, one has to conduct himself in a righteous manner. In order to teach honesty, one has to be honest. In order to teach morality, one has to exhibit strong moral judgment and behavior.

Were it this simple we could merely conduct ourselves in an ethically moral manner and never have to again worry about the integrity of the Black male youth. The other side of the problem is that society defines the parameters for establishing sound, ethically moral behavior and then sends our youth both the temptation and equipment to violate those very same parameters. When I say society, I mean local, state, and federal officials. I mean businesses, relatives, friends, and parents, including us. Society establishes teen curfews and then offers midnight basketball. Our congressmen write the laws of the land and then flood Washington with a sea of bad checks. Municipalities establish automobile speed limits and then allow the manufacturing and selling of radar detectors. Legislatures launch legal assaults on affirmative action, welfare, and minimum wage increases, adding to our youth's present state of hopelessness, then they supplement these assaults with more police officers and prisons. For some strange reason, society screams foul, that the Black male youth shows a lack of integrity.

As I stated earlier, our youth do not subscribe to the "do as I say, not as I do" philosophy. They learn by the examples shown to them, which is normal learning behavior. The temptations put forth by society, which include us, amount to entrapment. If I am correct in labeling this behavior by society as entrapment, entrapment then is also a process. It is a process instituted by repeated acts of inconsistency culminating in the experience necessary to give our youth the confidence to violate both legal and ethically moral parameters. If our youth were aware of the entrapment process, they would not fall victim to it. Their awareness of the entrapment process is our responsibility. Their awareness of the entrapment process is part of our commitment in their upbringing. The responsibility for this awareness is not to be taken as any easy task. The responsibility for teaching them integrity by practicing it should also not be considered the full extent of the task, for even more detrimental to our youth's well-being and integrity is their courage.

Youth in general, at least in the last fifty years, have exhibited an enormous amount of courage. They have held protests in America, China, and even South Africa, to name but a few. They aspire to the ideal and are responsible for great magnitudes of social change. Their courage is not to be questioned. If it is up for question, history will most certainly give it a vote of confidence.

For all practical purposes then, how far can we push the parameters of integrity? We can't; we are their teachers. They learn by our example. They learn from teachers, whose courage is now subverted by their responsibilities to home mortgages, car notes, and most importantly, their commitment to their youth.

Part of that commitment entails tightening our own parameters around the things we seek to get away with. If we seek to get away with driving violations, overcharged credit cards, overdrawn bank accounts, and late payments for this or that, I guarantee you that we will still lead them by example. We'll still set the example for our youth whose courage has not been tempered by the responsibilities of adulthood. We'll still set the example for an untempered courage that is destined by design to stretch those already extended parameters by an amount at least equal in strength to itself. This stretching of parameters is one of the areas where integrity ends and legal violations begin. Legal violations on a continuous basis become a historical process that always ends in sanctions. They are actions that history has taught us will always resurface to redeem themselves. If we buy that history does indeed redeem itself, we owe it to our youth to reduce and even eliminate our most minute temptations. For just as historical experience shows its ugly head to us, so it will to them. It will show itself to redeem tenfold the teaching of our actions upon the Black male youth, for he has shown that he has always had ten times our courage.

What they will perceive as a minor infraction is coupled with an unmitigated courage. One youth's minor infraction is considered a felony charge to a public official and so go the sanctions. This is quite a price for our youth to pay simply so that we may stretch restriction limits. If we stay exclusively within our preset bounds, perhaps our youth will not stray too far; perhaps the redemption price will be small.

However, we need to further reduce the redemption price for our youth's acceptance of the temptations of entrapment. We must communicate to them our acknowledgment of their courage. We must show them both sides, the accomplishments and the failures of that courage. Since it would be useless for us to question their courage, we must convince them to question it. We can do this by repeatedly showing them the pitfalls of the entrapment process as well as its sanctions. We must convince them that their courage must not be wasted on the frailties offered by the entrapment process, for to do this would be to expose that courage. We already know that any display of our youth's courage is to have them deemed a suspect. We must communicate to them that it takes a lot more courage to conceal one's courage. It takes a lot more courage to reserve the display of one's courage until one meets a task requiring that courage. It takes a lot more courage to maintain one's integrity when all around us no one is displaying integrity. It takes a lot more courage to do on a daily basis what is required to insure one's future. It takes an enormous amount of courage to be unmoved by peers', relatives', and society's temptations that are offered in advance of one's movement up history's spiral evolutionary ladder.

There will come a time for youth to display that courage. That time will come when our youth have to make the quantum leap from history's preparatory process to the level of development called greatness. At that point, there absolutely cannot be any questions pertaining to their integrity, for others may have to vouch for it. We see this vouching for one's integrity almost daily in presidential nominations for this or that. We also often see these opportunities for greatness shattered, not for lack of accomplishments but for lack of integrity. Whereas the nominees thought they had exhibited the courage to violate parameters set by those who define integrity, in all actuality they did not have the courage to resist the temptations of entrapment.

Our youth, at this juncture in their lives, cannot afford to waste their courage. It should be used only during crucial moments that could have a positive impact on their futures. It should never be used to impede their future.

Their courage is a given. It needs merely to be channeled along the same path that leads to their successful futures. The questions of integrity and courage are the flip sides of the same coin. Integrity requires courage to insure itself, and courage demands the support of integrity. Our youth require our guidance in the display of this courage. This display of courage must always surface on the same side as integrity. If we are not to teach them this, who is? We are to teach them that whenever true courage is displayed, there are never any regrets regardless of outcome, for true courage has the support of integrity. As in the student protests that I mentioned earlier, youth's courage was backed one hundred percent by their integrity, and their integrity had the full backing of their courage. Our youth's courage should always be backed by their integrity, and their integrity must always surface on the same side as their courage. Anything else amounts to entrapment. Our commitment to our youth demands that we show them the difference between the inseparable union of integrity and true courage and its opposite: entrapment (which gives the appearance of exhibiting courage but is most certainly lacking the element of integrity).

RAP MUSIC

It would make little sense to attempt addressing issues in the upbringing of the Black male youth without at least touching on rap music. I chose to not merely impose my personal observations on the subject but to also solicit the services of Ronald "G. Wiz" Butts. His experience on the subject matter includes disc jockeying for two St. Louis radio stations and a local skating rink, at least one recording, and direct contacts with a couple of national recording artists that have gone platinum and triple platinum, who incidentally presented him with a couple of trophies for his dedication and support of the music. In our interview, the very first question that I asked him was, "Why won't rap music go away?" Wiz's response was, "Why won't a baby in pain stop crying?" When asked to elaborate, it was revealed to me that rap music, like blues, rhythm and blues, rock, country and western, opera, and all other forms of music represent to its listeners the expression of the inner self. Wiz further stressed the point rather strongly that if you have any desire to know what the inner self wishes to express or acknowledge, listen to that person's music. Plain, simple, and right to the point.

This appeared to me to open a Pandora's box, because now we have more serious questions such as music depicting violence, drugs, strong sexual overtones, and blatant disrespect for women, all of which are accompanied by massive amounts of vulgarity.

Vulgarity first and foremost represents an expression form that the federal authorities allow. We all receive massive doses of it in the nineties through various forms of communication such as television, radio and newspapers. Now that youth have chosen to blend it, if you will, into an expression form (that is acceptable by the communication authorities), it represents a problem. Youth do not control the vehicles of communication, or anything else for that matter—adults do. They've merely applied this acceptable version of communication to their music.

Not having much of an argument that I could win against the communication authorities, I immediately switched to the content of rap music. Shifting gears back to the drugs, violence, and sexual overtones, I once again found myself being enlightened. The different aspects of rap music proved not to be stagnant music forms, nor did they prove to be standing in timeless isolation. Wiz explained to me that the rap music forms are part of the same evolutionary process that our music endured. His explanation made me realize that rap music follows the same historical cycles that began in our own music and that nothing new has been created other than the way it is expressed. Some of these historical cycles include:

1. (Rap) Bragging and boasting
   (Ours) "Agent Double-O-Soul"
2. (Rap) Afrocentric rap
   (Ours) "Say It Loud—I'm Black and I'm Proud"

3. (Rap) Black militancy
   (Ours) "Message From a Black Man"
4. (Rap) Gangster rap
   (Ours) "Trouble Man," "Superfly"
5. (Rap) Booty music
   (Ours) Go-go and disco music

They also have music depicting strong sexual content, and we have "Sexual Healing." Blatant disrespect for women has to be an outward reaction to the historical battle of the sexes (more on this shortly). This is a battle in which female rap artists now frequently strike back or internalize the disrespect by insisting on having a "roughneck."

Finally, Wiz revealed to me that rap music was also a method of interstate communication that, through lyrics, allows youth on the East Coast to know "what's in" on the West Coast, encompassing all cities in between.

In answer to my original question of "Why won't rap music go away?" it was also revealed that its appeal will remain strong primarily due to:

1. The beat
2. The substance and content (which we get somewhat into)
3. The hook line (catchphrase)
4. The generation (the age group that listens to and buys the music)
5. The underground (the route that music takes for survival; for instance, before parental advisory music was commercially acceptable, rap music was sold, bought, and played through non-public vehicles)

This book is being written in an attempt to salvage our Black male youth. They have problems that were generated by themselves, us, and society at large. The previous information on rap music is to neither reject it nor accept it, but if we don't cease refusing to acknowledge it as an "expressive" art form, we run the risk of not hearing what it is expressing. If our job is about commitment and preparation for their futures, I suggest that we better know who and what they view as friend and foe. We better know what makes them happy and what makes them sad. We better know what they feel is worth fighting for as well as what they feel should be discarded. If we ignore their innermost expressions, how can we undo what needs to be undone? What clues will we have to not tamper with those things that are in perfect harmony with their successful development? If we do want to know what may or may not need to be undone, the strongest clue is in their music, for their music is a reflection of them.

And yet there are elements in rap music that send out very strong signals that say "all is not well." There is Afrocentric rap that absolutely must exist, for society has said that we are nothing, and though America tries to ignore our contributions to this society, we will never allow this country to view us as invisible. Segments of the rap industry back us on these convictions, and they stand firm.

There is rap music that depicts black militancy, and again our youth reaffirm our convictions. They know that we must never lie down and accept being humiliated peacefully. Once again we must applaud them, for these contributions are in perfect harmony with their long-term well-being as well as ours.

Yet this art form also exhibits several reflexes that we vehemently object to. It gives us blatant disrespect for the Black female, gangster rap, and bragging and boasting, all of which have either evolved through historical processes or led to the evolution of other historical processes.

Segments of the rap industry graphically and blatantly disrespect the Black female. The Black female represents their future wives, our daughters, and the mothers of all future generations of Black heritage. The irony in such disrespect is that it is an acknowledgment of the disrespect for oneself. It is an acknowledgement that historically, Black males have not been able to provide for or protect our women and our babies. It is an acknowledgment that this segment of rap artists have internalized this auction block mentality, a mentality that dictates a viewpoint of nonattachment to one's family. This auction block mentality dictates that Black males become absentee biological fathers, for all Black babies are the responsibility of the slavery system, the welfare system, the food stamp system, and the system of Black male unemployment. For some of the rap artists, there are no other eyes to view the Black female through except those of contempt and disrespect.

At first it was clearly understood that the Black male must willingly allow himself to be sold into slavery or face death or dismemberment. It was understood that he must not attempt to protect his family lest he be boiled during his final public appearance. It was understood that he must not attempt to feed his family, for that might amount to stealing prior to having his hands amputated.

However, hundreds of years later boiling Black men and limb amputations are illegal, and the Black female resents heading fifty-three percent of all Black households. She resents having to raise Black babies with only meager jobs and meager assistance from the slave master. She resents the "player" mentality that she knows evolved from slavery as a breeding process. Yes, she resents the Black male boasting that he is a stud, for she understands that the stud evolved as property of the slave master, and as such he has no responsibilities. No, she does not hold the player, the stud, the absentee biological father in high esteem. She does not respect him because she cannot rely on him. Today, as in the past, he claims no responsibility except as a breeder. After breeding he must be discarded both physically and psychologically.

The Black male youth resents being resented. He resents being resented by the economic system, and he disrespects it. He resents being resented by the political system, and he disrespects it. Finally he resents being resented by the social system, and he disrespects it. He includes the Black female in the social system, and he disrespects her. The problem, however, is that she is not part of the social system. She is a victim of the social system, just as he is. For just as he was stripped of his parental responsibilities at the auction block of breeders, she was also stripped of his accepting his responsibilities, leaving behind only a breeder, a stud, and a player. Her babies were stripped of their father. Centuries later they're still fatherless.

So is it possible for this type of rap artist to disrespect the Black female without disrespecting himself? Is it possible for him to brag about being a stud or a player without disrespecting himself? If the Black female is the enemy, then he himself must be the enemy, for they are both the result of historical inhumane injustices.

Blatant disrespect for our women then becomes the result of the vicious cycle of a historically internalized auction block breeding mentality. This side of rap music will not go away until disrespect for one's self goes away. It will not dissolve until the player deems it more important to accept the responsibility of the protection and provisions of his family.

For then and only then will there be no resentment of the Black female's resentment and thus the disrespect because of it.

Next we have the "harmless" bragging and boasting about what I have and how "cool" I am. My cars, my clothes, my jewelry, and my women epitomize who I am. They are what I am, and they are all that I am. Bragging then exposes my lack of substance and my lack of historical experience, for if you remove my designer clothes and burn my luxury car (that I just missed my insurance payment on to buy the gold chain), I am nothing. There is no substance and there is no humanity, for all my humanity is at the jewelry store and the car dealership. Will I be able to keep my women with no designer shirts?

I know that I am trading my future for a name brand humanity, but it is the only humanity that I have, and it is essential that I keep it. My designer trinkets become my "cool," which is my humanity; therefore I must keep my "cool" by any means necessary. I will keep my "cool" even if it means destroying another's humanity or "cool" or whatever. I will take another's woman, for she is only after the "coolest" of "cools," which I am. Do not, however, attempt to violate my "cool." There will be no disrespect here, lest I pull the trigger. The trigger guards my "cool." Your humanity, your woman, your jewelry, and low-rider trucks are also part of my "cool," for I am the Mack, the Player President.

This is what bragging, boasting, and gangster rap reveals. It is an art form of honest expression. It is also an honest expression of self-denial. It is a denial of any self-worth outside of those things that make me "cool." It is a denial of any plans for the future including employment prospects, meaningful human relationships, and plans for the future of one's offspring.

After the gangster is gone, what is the legacy? The legacy is one of self-serving destruction of all in its path. And what exactly was in its path? The humanity of another? An innocent victim of a drive-by with no age discrimination? Certainly, but the legacy was also in its own way, for gangster style begets gangster style. My "dogs" versus your "dogs" equal "no dogs." Ultimately there will be triumph. Triumph to incarceration that requires cashing in my jewelry, cars, and designer clothes to defend my humanity against incarceration. Oops, I've just cashed in my humanity, which leaves no substance.

We parents of Black male youth absolutely must listen to our youth's music if we are to direct them in resolving their problems and ours, for the message is indeed in the music. The vulgar disrespect for our women, the bragging and boasting, and the gangster rap are telling stories of the past and present, thus making predictions for the future. Our youth are merely reacting to centuries of conditioning and inhumane conditions. These are conditions that we ourselves have internalized and passed on to them, for we were the players of yesteryear. As I said earlier, our youth have created nothing new. They may have modified, revised, and taken the music to a higher or lower level, whichever one you prefer, but they did not create the subject matter.

Our duty then is to take an objective (not reactive) view of their modified version of the subject matter, decipher its message, draw out the underlying historical concepts, and utilize them for their guidance. They cannot do this for themselves, for they are merely reacting to history. It is we that must teach them about the mirror images of auction block studding and the twenty-first century "player." We must teach them that their bragging and boasting is an escape mechanism to hide hopelessness. We must teach them that hopelessness always results in uncontrolled behavior and violence, for there is nothing else to lose. Bragging and boasting, when used as an expressive art form to hide hopelessness, must absolutely transcend into gangster rap, becoming the "coolest of the cool" by absorbing another's humanity by any means necessary (including murder). Finally we must teach them that even the idea of taking another's life to maintain one's cool has to be given up because the story, in order to be real, must always end in incarceration or death. It is our duty then to transpose the historical subliminal messages of their music into a language that they can understand. They sing them as reflex actions to conditions set in front of them; however, reflex actions have never been known to control themselves.

PUNISHMENT

Punishment represents another peculiar aspect of Black male child rearing. It is peculiar in the sense of determining where it falls in the best interest of adult life preparation. It is also peculiar in that it has to be determined where punishment as a tool for child-rearing ends and outright vengeance begins.

Is punishment justified in the case of an honest mistake, a one-time occurrence that does not happen to be a case of overt disobedience? I think not. What if the child or teen is testing our patience or authority? If he crosses the line in his testing of us, do we punish or spank him? Remember, this is a case of obvious disobedience. Or is it?

Why would our youth have a need to test us? Do they not know where we stand on the issue? Do they not know where we stand on all issues at all times? Do they not have a consistent line of historical experience on all our words, positions, and actions? Certainly they have. If our words, positions, and actions have been questionable and wavering to our youth in the past, they will be questionable and wavering to our youth in the present. If this is the case, we have created the need for our youth to test us, for they know not where we stand.

If we are wavering, our positions become questions that require answers. They become questions that our youth must resolve since we haven't. "How committed are Mom and Dad to their words? Will they waver or will they hold? I really want this bad, and I don't know where they stand. I'll test my luck. Since they may waver, I have at least a fifty-fifty chance. I'll do it anyway."

So he's crossed the line that we've drawn (this time). In our disciplinary action, we prescribe the usual punishments: no television, can't go outside, stay in their room, and no phone calls. Let's examine these sanctions briefly. They can't watch the same television that the "anti-television violence people" protest and object to for two weeks. So for two weeks, they have to cleanse their minds of "movie world filth." They can't go outside for two weeks to subject themselves to society's dangers, peer pressures, drive-by shootings, and policemen's suspicions. They must stay in their rooms that we, not they, pay the rent on, and get plenty of relaxation from the hustle and bustle otherwise known as the rat race. Finally, they cannot talk on the telephone spreading all types of teen gossip and conjuring up who knows what types of ill-conceived plans that are destined to backfire in their faces. And we expect this type of punishment to work. I believe the homeless would kill for this type of life.

In our eyesight, this is as close to imprisonment as we can imitate, but does adult life imprisonment even work? If we say that it does, how do we account for so many of our youth perpetuating acts that will result in imprisonment? How do we account for so many of our youth becoming repeat offenders? If I am correct in this assessment, even society has set the stage for their adulthood imprisonment, for society is wavering in its rules and authority; and those rules and that authority must be tested. Society wavers seriously in its commitment to anti-criminal activity.

Sure, they build more jails and spend in excess of twenty-five thousand dollars per year per inmate, but if offered freedom in exchange for their working a fifty-thousand-dollar-per-year job, you'd clean out the penal system. If offered the same job in exchange for their gang membership cards, we would have to open a nationwide cardboard recycling center.

Punishment, which the facts have shown, is worthless. It is equivalent to spitting on a gasoline fire. It's going to keep right on burning. The best way to prevent a gasoline fire is to keep gasoline and sparks separate. If the two should meet, you don't punish the gasoline fire by spitting on it. We do not eliminate unwanted behavior in our youth with worthless punishments. We should prevent the unwanted test of our authority by keeping our youth away from any wavering and inconsistent positions that we hold. Prevention is the cure. Repairing the damage is not the cure.

But sometimes the damage does have to be repaired, for if allowed to go unchecked, our youth will still wind up victims of a worthless penal institution. If not punishment, then what?

An unwavering position is a preventive measure. Repairing the damage must be accomplished through accountability. The damage must be repaired by the one that did it. As I stated earlier, any infraction requires repayment in work. If our sons were told not to go to a party and they went anyway and were gone for five hours, they owe the household five hours of work, plus a couple of hours for the blatant violation of household rules. An even exchange is no swindle.

I cannot, however, overemphasize consistent, unwavering positions on our part. Anything else amounts to creating questions that must be answered, which again amounts to entrapment. Our goal is not to trick or entrap our youth but to prepare them. If they understand our positions, they will understand their own. As I stated earlier, youth create nothing. They may modify and they may change, but they create nothing. It is all learned behavior. We must teach them where we stand on all issues. We must be unwavering on all matters. We must eliminate their need to test us, thereby eliminating the need for punishments. Only then does the question of accountability come into play. Consistent behavior on our part produces consistent behavior on theirs.

YOUTH SAVINGS

First of all, I don't want to assume that our youth have anything to save. This is determined solely on the basis of whether there's anything to spend. Video games, basketball shoes (if used mainly for fashion), and a host of other trendy trinkets would imply that there is money to spend. If he has an oversupply of any of these, I would say he has money to save. "What's the big deal on saving?" We say, "He's only a child; let him enjoy his childhood." The big deal is that savings become even more critical for our youth that are used to having things.

For them to wake up one morning and not have is to be in a state that is synonymous with poverty. I know that "synonymous with poverty" may sound a bit extreme, but let's look at it. The kid that has had it all looks up one day and has to wear the no-name brand shoes, still has the older outdated video games, and does not have any of the latest trendy trinkets, then soon falls out of grace with his peers. These are the things by which they measure acceptance and rejection. Now we say, "Then they weren't true friends anyway." Perhaps not. Nevertheless, those trinkets are what they had in common. Superficial as it may sound, reality has it that the rich don't hang out with the poor, winners don't hang out with losers, the successful don't hang out with failures, and the haves don't hang out with the have nots. I am not attempting to condone name-brand trinkets but to merely point out the psychological impact of going from being one of the haves to one of the have nots.

To fall from grace among one's peers is to fall into the spaciousness of isolation, rejected by peers and also rejected by those that were previously rejected. This area of isolation makes youth susceptible to all types of vulnerabilities, for now what was really important comes to the forefront. It's not the trinkets, it never was. It is acceptance that was sought after. It always was, but who will accept them now? Who's left? Gangs? Drug users? Drug dealers? Who knows. The kid that spends every dime he gets his hands on is the kid that has no concept of his future. His spending is essentially out of control with no eye toward tomorrow. He believes that there is always more where that came from. He believes that Momma and/or Daddy will always have a job. We must question very seriously where he came up with those beliefs. Many of us believed that there was more where we got our last paycheck. We soon found ourselves walking right into a recession that required corporate downsizing. We also found that we had to forgo our next purchase. In addition to that, we found that we had to forgo some of our previous purchases, which included an assortment of trendy trinkets, our automobiles, and finally our homes.

If our spending habits were anything like those of our youth that spent everything he got his hands on, we probably also overextended our credit. We knew we had an endless supply of paychecks coming. When the economy proved us wrong and we lost our jobs along with our credit, and since we had already spent everything, we lost our dignity. We soon fell out of grace with our peers. So it goes with our youth; it is one and the same.

Those that don't heed history's warnings are doomed to repeat it. Money and spending are also part of a historical cycle. It is called an economic cycle. Don't think for a minute that our youth are not a part of this process. If they weren't, advertisers wouldn't spend billions of dollars trying to get their few, since it seems that what is true for us is also true for our youth. It is our job as parents to instill a savings habit in them now. It is our job to make sure they avoid the financial ruin that many of us have experienced at one time or another. If we have been consistent in our commitment and our actions, they will trust our judgment. After a prolonged process of consistent saving, he will begin to feel financially confident with or without the trendy trinkets, for if he has the cash, they are always readily available, which reduces the urgency. Who knows, he may be able to pay the rent during the next recession. It is coming.

DRUGS

Drug usage in our youth represents a perception problem for us. The essence of this problem is that due to drugs' mind-altering effects, we cannot know whether our youth are in full or even partial control of their faculties. The mind has been altered. We know not whether to trust their motor skills, their sense of judgment, or their ethical and moral value systems. It matters little whether our youth started out on the soft stuff and progressed to the more serious habits. It makes even less sense to qualify the destructive impact of this drug versus that drug. What does matter is first, the stage of addiction or usage, and second, their commitment level to the entire drug scene. The importance of this is so that we can make a concerted effort to repair the damage and preventive measures that we parents must take to stop even the initiation into the world of drugs.

Drug usage can represent a phase of kicks, escapism, or outright addiction, and even though we parents may or may not be directly responsible for an environment in which our youth would seek kicks or escapism, we are certainly responsible for their well-being, and drugs are not a part of it. Drug usage would be a part of their demise. That demise has its own historical cycle. It could start out, as I said, as kicks or just something to do. This kicks phase, once entered into, quickly reveals a mental dimension in which there are no cares, no problems, and no concerns such as homework, parental pressures, or future job prospects. What started out as just something to do has shown itself to be a self-fulfilling prophecy. Kicks now offer admission into a theater of escape from the world's problems (right there in the comfort of their own minds). There is no worry for the seemingly hopeless state of futuristic employment prospects. There is no worry to actualize one's human potential. There is no worry to concern themselves with seemingly abstract concepts such as confidence, integrity, or greatness. And yet the world goes on. By their very acknowledgment of seeking temporary escapism, they also acknowledge the world and their presence in it. Still, each and every time they seek kicks or escapism, they make serious withdrawals from their bank accounts of human potential. They withdraw, and it diminishes. They withdraw again, and it diminishes further. They withdraw yet again, and now it is near depletion. Things that used to matter, or that could matter, or that should matter, now become a back seat priority. Back seat priorities get done if and when they get to them. Nine times out of ten, it's if they get to them. Pretty soon, "if" will not even be a question. All drive has been drained in the name of kicks and escapism, which have now become the priority—a priority whose name is addiction—and the prophecy has fulfilled itself. The escapist world is now real, and the real world is now the fantasy world that the addicted hopes to escape to.

 This stage of drug usage called addiction represents the ultimate episode in the usage cycle. It has its own individual death cycle and manifests itself in the actual movement of the living dead. Their character is deceptive only to nonusers, who often make misinformed value judgments on the addicted. Some say that he doesn't want to get help and calls him a worthless junkie. Others say that they know he can kick the habit and that deep down inside, he's really a good person. Only the addict knows that he is outside of any valid judgment calls on his character. He knows that until the actual addiction is completely conquered, neither his intentions nor his will matter, for the addiction is just that, an addiction. It is responsible for the selling of many items of value for pennies. It is responsible for many missing items and innumerable crimes including purse snatching, car theft, burglaries, and even murder. All too often it is even responsible for self-induced death. We err seriously when we make judgment calls on the character of the addict. His relationship to us falsely guides us to think that he is merely in a bad state of mental disarray. Addiction is not, and I repeat, is not a state of mind. It is a state of being. Perhaps it is a psychological state of being. Perhaps it is a physical state of being, or both. It is a state of being that to nonusers is synonymous with irresponsibility, and yet the question of responsibility cannot enter its realm.

Drug usage represents the first of two possible commitments to the drug world. We have all heard that the best cure for any ailment is prevention, and this is also true in regard to drug usage. As I stated earlier in respect to the significant other, our youth are seeking answers to both simple and perplexing questions. Our commitment is to provide those answers. We have to provide functional answers and functional solutions and approaches to their problems. We have to make them understand that they have untapped reserves in the embodiment of human potential. We have to make them understand that any mountain can be climbed or chipped away at through repetition that adds to experience and culminates in confidence. We have to make them know that the legitimate excuse—that is, the unpassable mountain—is an unacceptable barrier to be overcome through the usage of the aforementioned tools. To do anything less is to allow them to view adversity and obstacles as entities to be avoided and ran from; and what is avoiding and running from if not escapism and thus an open invitation that justifies drug usage. Once this justification is internalized, the drug usage scenario can begin to unfold.

What if we are too late and drug usage has already begun? Just as I stated earlier, during drug usage, we err seriously when we attempt to make valid judgment calls on a user's character. So it goes with attempting to make judgment calls on the level of commitment to drug usage. I think that we are at least in agreement that drugs are an awesome evil and must be dealt with. I don't think, however, that most of us are equipped and competent enough to administer cures. If we do suspect drug usage, we should not take it lightly. Seek whatever professional and community help is available. Just as we commit to our youth when they are doing well, be just as committed when they are doing bad. Just as we would not abandon our youth if they had muscular dystrophy, do not abandon them now. See the sickness through. Remember, hopelessness played a big part in this situation. Do not generate more. The second part of our youth's possible involvement in the drug world has to do with its commercial side. Its consequences and repercussions are equally as dangerous. Just as in the usage cycle, dealing drugs has its own death cycle. We have all seen it. Sell a bit. Buy some toys, go to jail. If said dealer does not go to jail, he expands his territory (or gets killed trying to expand or trying to collect). If he expands, he gets big enough to be noticeable and then he goes to jail (or dies because of the expansion).

For me to say that we should turn our drug-dealing youth over to the authorities would be a useless request, for they are a part of us, and we wouldn't do it anymore than we would turn ourselves in. Yet we'd better address this issue as if his very life depends on it, because it does.

If he doesn't cease dealing in drugs, he may die now or he may die later, but he will die. Historical experience says it's so. It is our duty to show him this history, for it has made him a target for death now and in the future. His expensive cars, clothes, and other trendy trinkets have put the spotlight on him, making him visible to any number of predators, and as any predator would do, they seek the easy prey. They seek the one in the open. They seek the one most visible. They seek the one that appears to be the weakest and the one that doesn't have the experience of survival. This would be our drug-dealing youth. They have not internalized the historical experience of drug dealing. They do not see themselves as the victims of drug-related gangster-style murders. They do not see themselves as the victims of extortion by policemen on the take. They do not see themselves as the envy of those that wish they had what they have. They do not see themselves as robbery targets by those that haven't the slightest clue as to who they are. Yet they have a spotlight shining on them.

These are merely some of the reasons why we as parents of Black male youth must give them a historical perspective. We must not allow them to become victims of the very same historical process that they seek to outwit. Neither they nor we can outwit history, for history is what we make it. Each and every one of us is made up of our own history, and it would be useless to try to outwit ourselves. Show them the history that they are building. If nothing else, build them a historical experience from newspaper clippings. If I am correct, it will be no problem to show the rise, fall, and total demise of familiar names and faces involved in drug dealing. Show them the deaths of familiar names and faces involved in drug dealing. Show them the incarceration of familiar names and faces involved in drug dealing. Show them this history and its inevitable outcome, or bury them.

INDIVIDUALISM AND HISTORICAL PERSPECTIVE

We are all reared in a society geared toward individual rights and respect for other people's opinions. The concept of individuality is well grounded throughout our every fiber. During casual conversation and even serious debate, the phrase "To me..." can be heard justifying our positions. We purchase individual servings of this and individual servings of that. We are so individualized that we consider the individual to be the whole. Another way of saying this is that we consider the part to be the whole, that reality in its entirety is from our perspective.

What's the big deal, and how does this impact our youth's upbringing? Let's examine this harmless internalized concept. To start, individualism in its commercialized form convinces us that it is worth the extra cost to pay more for individual servings. It is worth the extra cost to pay more for less. What a voluntary waste of our few resources.

In our individuality, we have learned to respect the individual's opinion, so it is alright to justify a position being debated with "To me" this is what is important, or "I feel..." In essence what we have done is taken all of reality, placed it on a shelf, and then created a new reality from within our own limited experience. The danger in this is that we ignore objective reality and put our own subjective individuality in its place. Because of this mindset we will be forever barred from utilizing historical experience. We will be forever barred from ever obtaining greatness. As individuals, we will be doomed to ignore history's warnings. We will be doomed to repeat mistakes that have already been made. "It didn't happen to me; that's not my experience. I don't believe that it could happen to my kids. It hasn't so far."

This is a very dangerous viewpoint because our every action or refusal to act is based on our beliefs. For instance, if we believe four quarters are equivalent to one dollar and we're seeking change for a dollar in quarters, we demand four quarters. If we believe that the corner store only gives three quarters for a dollar, we will go elsewhere. If we believe that there is a random shooting right outside our front door, we will not open it. If we believe our neighbors mean us great harm, we will adjust our behavior accordingly. We act or refuse to act based only on our beliefs. If we rule out the possibilities of failure, drug addiction, and gang membership that are engulfing our youth, we will not be on guard to fend off these misfortunate situations. When symptoms of failure, drug addiction, and gang membership do show up, we won't see them initially because we have ruled out their possibility. Yet all the symptoms are there. "It's been three weeks since my child has had any homework, but he's a straight-A student, so I rule out his possibility of failure." "My kid has been withdrawn lately and things are coming up missing, but he could not be on drugs because he's always helped me pay the bills." "My teen now stays out very late with his new friends and they all dress alike, but he couldn't be in a gang. He's the president of the church choir."

All the symptoms are there, but because of our individualistic beliefs, our youth are quickly deteriorating. What else would a symptom be if not history in the making? Every time symptoms appear (repetition), they add to the experience that makes for future failure, drug addiction, or gang membership. When we do acknowledge our youth's situations, it's an uphill battle, for we have ignored the symptoms. We have ignored history in the making. Like any sickness, the quicker its symptoms are diagnosed, the easier the cure. If we continue to ignore the symptoms, we'll have a full-blown terminal disease.

Those that sidestep the individualistic perspective and view others' mistakes as having the possibility of being their own are able to avoid the mistakes without the personal setback. Those that step outside of individuality's parameters and view others' errors and advances as their own experiences are able to go toward new achievements and greatness. Those that are truly great may start out at the beginning, but soon they learn to internalize others' maximum experiences. They soon learn to internalize even the experiences of those that they view as great. What they do not do is to stifle their learning with their own personalized experiences.

Certainly there is individuality. America is predicated upon it, and we hope that it always will be. However, when our youth's individuality begins to stifle their development, we must step in and show them that the parts make up the whole and that there can be no whole with any one part standing in isolation. There can be no successful team even with all individual superstars unless they work in unison. There can be no monumental achievements unless history's previous works are taken into account.

And yet in their own way, our youth almost instinctively reject the individualistic perspective. They acknowledge this by their involvement with peers and even gangs. Man is a social creature, and even our youth want to be a part of something whole. They resort to individualistic behavior for selfish ends only. Even the system that espouses this individuality deals with our youth as a group with anti-affirmative action assaults, anti-minimum wage assaults, and proposed legislation for carrying concealed weapons to protect themselves from criminals (another group).

Our youth absolutely must be made to see that the whole is made up of the sum of its parts. Even the individual acts of repetition are what form experience. One act can be either a good act or a bad act, but all the individual acts are what give the action its overall character. Then and only then does justifiable confidence manifest itself in pursuing the action.

Do not allow our youth to indulge in individualistic behavior to the detriment of their long-term well-being and growth. Some of us have lived or learned enough to have a functional knowledge of historical experience and can see future results from symptoms. We have been lucky enough to learn from our own experiences as well as from others'. We do all the fitting and necessary things to help our youth both survive and grow. However, as fate would have it, our peers are not always that fortunate, and their youth begin to show symptoms of long-term detrimental behavior, such as temper tantrums, persistent begging after they've been told no, and talking back to their parents. We see these symptoms and somehow convince ourselves that their parents see the long-range consequences. We convince ourselves of their knowledge because the facts are all around them. They had an older son that displayed the same behavior and he wound up dead or in the penitentiary. It's just not possible that they could be this blind, and we say, "They know" and do not intervene.

This is absolutely irresponsible behavior on our part for a couple of reasons. First, if we want to make sure their kid does not wind up in the penitentiary for let's say killing some other kid, we cannot assume the kid's parents have any insight into historical experience. If they did, they would see the pattern. They would believe their kid was headed toward doom. Then, as any parents would do, they would take the appropriate measures of prevention.

Secondly, how can we assume that any Black people have a historical perspective when our history has been erased? We have yet to build ourselves a meaningful history, so how can we be expected to have perspective on something that has never existed? Historical perspective is an outlook, a way of seeing and approaching reality. If your friends don't see the long-range consequences of their youth's actions, you must conclude that they don't have the insights that you have. There can be no other conclusion. At this point, it becomes your duty and mine to assist his parents in obtaining that perspective. Without historical perspective in his parents, he is doomed to repeat history. He is doomed to the full-blown consequences of his unguided, unmitigated actions, for his behavior will only become more and more detrimental. Salvaging our Black male youth does not stop at our own individual child. Black male youth are a group, and if we are to redirect them toward a more meaningful future, we must, of course, start with our own and then reach out wherever necessary.

CONCLUSION

There is no conclusion, for there has been no beginning. Immediately following our supposed emancipation, the shackles were removed and we were free. Free to wander aimlessly in pursuit of happiness. We were pursuing happiness with no foundation and no base to draw from. There was no foundation for support. There was no financial support, no psychological support, no historical support, no support period. As a result of starting from scratch, we had no choice but to try different things. We tried back to Africa movements, Christianity, and Islam. We supported both Democratic and Republican parties. We even placed our faith in a Black president. All these trails met with varying degrees of success, as well as the disappointments of failure. All these ventures initially offered hope. All of them have failed us miserably as solutions for the entire race. In our directionless quest to undo America's historical misdeeds, we missed the lesson of the ant and the grasshopper. We missed the fact that we must prepare today if we are to be assured tomorrow. There was no historical reason for us to prepare. For centuries, all tomorrow brought was pain. In our aimlessness, we missed preparing for our own future generations. There was no reason to conceive of future generations, for they often amounted the auction block. Not only have we missed preparing for our own future generations, but we have also missed preparing our youth for theirs. We gave them nothing, no foundation, no base of support. Now we have a repeated script in the Black male youth. He is running around aimlessly in pursuit of his happiness. Only this time he is not choosing Christianity or Islam. He is not choosing Democratic or

Republican party politics. He is choosing robbery, murder, drugs, gangs, and who knows what else. This is how he pursues happiness.

Removal of one's history is one of the worst crimes that could ever be inflicted upon a man. It will set him back a thousand years. But removing his history and then convincing him that he is normal is the ultimate deception in master trickery. It is in effect equivalent to blindfolding him, convincing him that he can see, and then encouraging him to walk the road of life. He cannot know where he's going because he does not know where he's been. To suggest that he head due north will result in even more confusion, for he knows not where south, east, and west lie. He will not be able to give his relatives and friends direction because he himself is lost. He will not be able to protect them because he is blindfolded and does not recognize danger when it confronts him. If he is a man of courage, however, he will lash out at anything that he feels will inflict harm upon him. In his blindness, he will attack anyone near, including friends, relatives, and neighbors. This is especially escalated when they are all blindfolded, for now we have mass confusion.

What is even more horrifying is that they will all trust those issuing the blindfolds. They always seem to offer a glimpse of light and a blind man's walking cane. They offer direction and point everyone not due north but always thirty degrees to the right or thirty degrees to the left. Some will stumble upon due north, but most will miss the mark. Those that wind up due south will be in a homicidal murderous rage with intentions of taking no prisoners.

Our youth are winding up due south. We must remove our blindfolds in order to direct them. We must remove their blindfolds and dismiss the blind man's walking cane. We must show them all four directions. They must have reference points from which to start. We must become the ones worthy of their trust. We must be the only ones they listen to for directions. The lines of communication established by those that removed the history may not be sufficient. They may not be designed for those with the missing history. If those that have blindfolded us in the past have something positive to offer, great. However, all offerings must come through the scrutiny of our historical experience. For us, a new caneless way of walking has to be established. With the removal of the blindfolds, we must be able to see further. We must be able to offer direction to friends and relatives. In other words, a new history has to be born and acknowledged. Every day and every moment of our youth's lives create that history. It is up to us to guide and nourish this history, and the time to start is now. We must train them in the examination and use of sound judgment, for they are the ones that will be making the decisions for their generation. They must also lay any foundations for future generations. They have the courage. They have the energy. They have the desire. We must be their foundation. We must guide them.

We must point them due north, replacing blindfolds and canes with historical experience and systematic confidence-building tools. We must teach ourselves and then teach the Black male youth to focus on their dreams, for their dreams are not subject to affirmative action or corporate downsizing. We must teach them the pitfalls of entrapment so as to avoid the accountability process. We must teach them how authority works as well as its direct relationship to entrapment. We must teach them about their courage and that it is only true courage when it is united with integrity. We must teach them all this and much more. We must test and retest these teachings and all other principles to ensure that they are consistent with a positive outlook for future prospects. This can only be done by sending our youth out into the real world and evaluating the results upon their return. If they have not succeeded in learning the sought after lessons, we may have to rethink our methods of training, retrain them, and send them back out into reality until they get it right. This is how adulthood emancipation must start. This is the path that the Black male youth must travel. And though they will be a far cry from any final conclusion, at tleast, we will have started a meaningful beginning.

Thank you.

www.ingramcontent.com/pod-product-compliance
Lightning Source LLC
LaVergne TN
LVHW012030060526
838201LV00061B/4539